Letters to Parents

JOHN RAE

LETTERS TO PARENTS

How to Get the Best Available
Education for Your Child

HarperCollins*Publishers*

HarperCollins*Publishers*
77–85 Fulham Palace Road,
Hammersmith, London W6 8JB

Published by HarperCollins*Publishers* 1998
1   3   5   7   9   8   6   4   2

The Author asserts the moral right to
be identified as the author of this work

A catalogue record for this book
is available from the British Library

ISBN 0 00 255695 2

Set in Sabon by Rowland Phototypesetting Limited
Bury St Edmunds, Suffolk

Printed and bound in Great Britain by
Caledonian International Book Manufacturing Ltd, Glasgow

To my granddaughter
Bronwyn

CONTENTS

PART TWO   CONSIDERING A SCHOOL

PART THREE   ASSESSING THE NON-ACADEMIC ASPECTS
             OF A SCHOOL

INTRODUCTION

The idea for this book stemmed from discussions I have had with our children about the education of *their* children. The scramble to get the best available education for your child is more hectic for them than it ever was for us. Why this should be so and what this new generation of parents should do about it are the subjects of these letters.

In the first part, I have concentrated on the importance of having a strategy. In the remaining three parts, I have tried to cover every possible aspect of choosing the right school. As each letter stands on its own there may inevitably be some repetition, but I have tried to keep this to a minimum.

The need for a strategy is something which baffles visitors from other countries. Surely, they say, you send your children to the local school like everyone else. If only it were that simple. I doubt whether parents anywhere else in the world have to agonize so much about their children's schooling. Britain is not alone in worrying about low standards of education, but it is alone in having such a complicated maze of good schools and bad schools, state schools and independent schools, day schools and boarding schools, single sex and co-ed schools; not to mention state schools that have opted out of local authority control, and independent schools that offer scholarships and bursaries to children of parents on low incomes.

What makes the parents' task even more difficult is that our assumptions about what constitutes a good school, and where good schools are to be found, are changing. The great divide in British education is not between state schools and independent schools, but between good schools and bad schools. For generations, the British believed that independent schools (or 'public schools' as they used to be called) were superior to state schools. Paying fees guaranteed a better education. By superior, the British did not necessarily mean academically superior; rather that the independent schools were thought to confer on their pupils a social cachet that would give them an advantage in adult life.

Now all that is changing. Academic results, not social cachet, are what parents are looking for. The best independent schools may lead the academic league tables, but the best state schools – particularly those that have opted out of local authority control – are not far behind.

There is a great deal more to education than academic results, but the league tables have raised doubts about whether some independent schools give parents value for money. These doubts focus on those boarding schools which figure prominently in the lower reaches of the league tables. If their academic results are poor and their social cachet counts for little today, what exactly do they offer for the fees they charge?

Faced with a complex and changing pattern of schools, parents recognize that their child's chances of a good education will depend on the skill and determination with which they plan and carry out their strategy. The stakes are high. The haves and have-nots in twenty-first century Britain will be those who have had a good education and those who have not. Forget the silver spoons. The privileged children will be those whose parents have got their educational act together.

The success of an educational strategy largely depends on the parents' ability to select the right school for their child. It is not an exact science. When all the information has been gathered, questions asked and visits made, the choice of school is still a gamble. Therefore, the purpose of the letters in parts two, three and four is to help parents improve the odds.

I have concentrated on secondary schools because they are the ones which provide hard evidence of the quality of education on offer, and because I think the choice of secondary school is the key to a successful overall strategy.

Many of the letters are about independent schools. Parents who can afford to pay fees are in a stronger position to exercise choice and in the independent sector they have a greater diversity of schools to choose from. But choice – real, not theoretical – is also expanding in the state sector, where good secondary schools that have opted out of local authority control are now able to recruit pupils from further afield. A new breed of parents are choosing to apply for a state school some distance from home because they like its standards and ethos. Other letters, therefore, are addressed to these parents, as well as to parents who are trying to make up their mind between a state school and an independent school. And, of course, there are letters in response to questions that apply equally to state and independent schools. On the question of bullying, for example, all parents have the same concerns and are just as keen to know what a school's policy on the subject is.

The letters contain advice and information as well as insights into how schools operate. This is not intended as a reference book, but it does suggest which state and independent schools have qualities – and not just academic qualities – that make them stand out from the rest.

Headteachers are very reluctant to acknowledge publicly that some schools are better than others, perhaps because that would be to admit that some headteachers are better than others. The official attitude of their organizations, such as the Headmasters' and Headmistresses' Conference (HMC), is that comparisons between schools are invidious because no two schools start from the same base. Unofficially, however, heads seek favourable publicity for their school and regard the misfortune of their rivals with quiet satisfaction.

This official standpoint is understandable and helps to sustain the pretence that schools are not competing directly with one another. But, from the parents' point of view, what some schools do better than others is vital information. The publication of academic league tables enables parents to see for the first time what heads fought long and hard to prevent them seeing, how schools compare in examination performance. But parents want to know much more than this.

At the risk of incurring the wrath of my former colleagues, the letters identify which schools I think are better than others and in what respect. These are personal judgements based on the available evidence. They are also provisional judgements because schools change for better or worse whenever there is a change of management. The best schools have a momentum of their own, but even these schools can decline with surprising speed if a weak headmaster or headmistress is appointed. Less well-established schools are acutely vulnerable to bad leadership.

Parents must, therefore, make their own assessment at the time of the schools they are interested in, remembering that reputations – both good and bad – can linger on after the justification for them has disappeared. These letters about schools are in effect a guide book to a country that may in some respects look different when you get there, but a book in which the advice on how to find your way around holds good.

Wherever possible I use the term head rather than headmaster or headmistress. If the former appears more often among the examples I give, it is because my own experience was as the headmaster of boys' schools.

In the course of writing this book I was helped by many people, not least the heads of state and independent schools. I am grateful to all of them. I am particularly grateful to my former colleague, Ann Hanks, who typed out the first draft and to Lucinda McNeile of HarperCollins for her unfailing encouragement and helpful criticism.

Part One

DEVELOPING A STRATEGY

1   What do we need to know before we start to plan our child's education?

Dear Dr and Mrs Attwood

You need to know what is happening to schools – who's up, who's down – and, more importantly, why our assumptions about what constitutes a good school and where those good schools are to be found are changing. You don't need to be experts on educational reform, but you do need to understand what has fuelled the many changes of recent years and how the different types of school have been affected.

People will disagree about what the most important changes are, but if I had to isolate one essential difference between our attitude to schools now and at any time over the last hundred years, I would say simply, academic success matters.

It has always mattered to some individuals and to some schools, but increasingly it is the yardstick by which all individuals and schools are measured. Don't be misled by reports of graduate unemployment during the recession. The well-educated will always have the edge in the job market. For schools, too, nothing succeeds like success. Good academic results increase demand which enables a school to be more selective, which in turn raises the academic standard still further.

There are individuals who can cock a snook at academic qualifications, just as there are schools – Gordonstoun and Millfield in the independent sector come to mind – that attract parents precisely because they refuse to let the pursuit of

4 Letters to Parents

academic success distort their broader view of education. But they are the exceptions.

Academic standards loom so large in parental calculations that it is easy to forget how recent this change is. I cannot put an exact date on it. I saw the first signs of change in the 1960s, but the full impact is only being felt thirty years later. Ambitious parents of modest means have long recognized that doing well in exams was the best way for their children to have the opportunities that wealthier families took for granted. But academic qualifications were not much prized in society as a whole or in the schools, where the swot was more likely to be bullied than praised and many teachers were more inclined to identify with the athletes than the scholars. Many middle-class parents regarded academic success with suspicion and of less value to their children than the non-academic benefits of a 'proper, public school education'.

To get on in the world, their children (particularly their sons) needed qualities of character, above all the willingness to take on the sort of responsibility that distinguishes the leaders from the led, the officers from the other ranks.

How dated the language sounds, but that is a measure of how far the pendulum has swung away from the traditional view of what public school education is about; a view which permeated the whole education system, so that the product of the excellent state grammar schools sometimes felt they had to apologize for having been to a school that took academic matters seriously.

What caused the pendulum to swing? I think the key to the answer is the expansion of the universities and the standardizing of university entrance based on A level grades. We are talking about the 1960s. Among the first to wake up to the implications of this were the leading independent schools. Oxford and Cambridge might retain their own entrance exam for a time, but parents who paid fees would increasingly come to expect schools such as Eton and Westminster to put their pupils in the strongest possible position for entry to all universities; and that meant good A levels for all, not just scholarships for a few.

In the 1970s, long before league tables appeared, the pursuit of academic success changed the culture of these schools. The old guard on the staff, I remember, fought hard against the emergence of what they regarded as the antithesis of a good education. They lost because – if you will forgive the phrase – you can't buck the market. Anyway, they were wrong. What was being rejected was not education for its own sake, but a failure to develop the potential of all the pupils.

The irony is that just as the leading independent schools were starting to take academic results seriously, most of the state schools were being encouraged to do the opposite. It was as though the two types of school had changed roles, the independent schools adopting the priorities of the grammar schools and the comprehensive schools turning against academic success.

That is another story, but if you wonder why independent schools dominate the top half of the academic league tables, it is not just a question of selection and resources; the more far-sighted independent schools read the signs of the times more accurately than those responsible for the state schools.

The swing of the pendulum gathered momentum throughout the 1980s and was given an extra push by the Conservative education reforms at the end of that decade. There is no sign of it being reversed. The chances are that your children will be educated in a climate in which academic success matters and it is essential, therefore, to plan your strategy with this in mind.

There is also another powerful current changing schools and affecting the choices open to your children, and that is the application of market forces to education. The theory is simple enough. If state schools are under-performing, force them to compete with one another for customers, as independent schools do, and they will soon raise their standards. In practice, the result appears to have been that the good schools get better and the bad schools get worse. There are more good state schools now, but they are still few and far between – and in some areas there are none at all.

There are about 4000 state secondary schools of which perhaps 1 per cent to 2 per cent perform consistently well in the A level league tables. Will that number increase before your children reach secondary school age? There is a good chance that it will. Of all the Conservative government reforms of the last decade – the national curriculum, local management of schools, league tables, city technology colleges – it was the introduction of so-called grant maintained schools that has increased the number of good state schools. These schools have been allowed to opt out of local authority control and are instead maintained by a grant from central government. The advantage being that they have greater freedom to decide what sort of school they want to be, and that many are academically selective in all but name.

One thousand secondary schools, or one quarter of the total, have opted for grant maintained status. Not all of them have achieved even a walk-on part in the academic league tables, but their academic standards are rising because that is what parents want. New Labour is ambivalent towards these schools but is unlikely to force them back under local authority control.

The best grant maintained schools and the state grammar schools that survived the 1960s are not yet challenging the best independent schools at the top of the league tables. Every year, however, more and more schools for which you do not have to pay fees are appearing in the top two hundred, with academic results that are better than the *majority* of independent schools.

The heads of independent schools, weeping crocodile tears over the iniquities of their privileged position, used to say that they would welcome competition from the state schools. Now their wishes are beginning to be granted. The emphasis on academic success has produced a situation where for the first time state and independent schools are competing for the same market and parents no longer assume that they have to pay fees to guarantee their children a good education.

In addition, as the number of good state schools is increasing, the number of good independent schools is falling. This is primarily because only a few of the existing boarding schools, which once dominated the independent sector, can meet the new parental expectations for academic success. Here, too, market forces appear to be making the good schools better and the bad ones worse.

The leading boarding schools, such as Eton and Winchester for boys and Wycombe Abbey and Cheltenham Ladies College for girls, are academic powerhouses and good all-round schools. But boarding schools in the lower half of the league tables, unless they have something special to offer, such as a strong religious ethos or skill in helping less able pupils, are in trouble and it would be a mistake to send your children to one of them even if you could afford the fees.

The heads of these boarding schools blame the recession for the shortfall of pupils, but they deceive themselves. The good boarding schools will survive, but boarding as a way of life for the middle classes has surely gone for ever. Once the pendulum had swung decisively in favour of academic success, the less-academic boarding schools that had traded successfully under the banner of 'public school' were doomed. The snobbery that equated boarding school with public school and public school with good school cuts no ice with today's generation of parents.

The leadership of the independent sector is passing to the fiercely-academic, single-sex day schools. They are much in demand because for many parents with high expectations for their children they represent the educational ideal – meritocratic, competitive and classless.

The gap between rising expectations and the inability of most schools to satisfy them is what fuels the intense debate about children's education which is such a feature of family life in this country. I see no sign of that situation changing, and I have no faith whatsoever in the ability of politicians and educationalists to produce in the foreseeable future an education system in which the majority of local state schools are good enough.

So you are going to have to plan carefully, and maybe to fight hard to secure a good education for your children. Having no illusions about that is the first step towards developing a successful strategy.

Yours sincerely
John Rae

2 What are the essentials of a successful strategy?

Dear Alyce

The first essential is to be single minded. You are planning your own children's education, so try not to let yourself be distracted by what is happening to other people's children. Some parents get so worked up about what they see as the injustices of the system that they use more energy inveighing against these than they do ensuring that their own children make the best of what is available.

The second is to be well informed. We all choose schools on the basis of insufficient information because prospectuses, anecdotes and league tables cannot tell us all we need to know. But we could be better informed than we usually are.

The third essential is to be flexible. Being single-minded does not mean pinning all your hopes on one school. Good schools have competitive entries; make sure you have checked out the alternatives. Your children's needs may be as difficult to assess as the schools you have in mind for them. Therefore, your strategy must be flexible enough to accommodate your changing perceptions of both.

Finally, it is essential to start planning early. Parents move into the catchment area of a good school before the baby is born and no doubt, in some cases, before the child is conceived. Although parents no longer put their child's name down for an independent school at birth, you do need to check when it is both advisable and possible to make sure his or her name has been registered. The same is true of popular state primary schools. Most parents who think in terms of a strategy probably start planning seriously when their child is three. This system seems extraordinary to people from other countries, yet in this country good education is not a right but a prize. Being rich does not guarantee your child is a prize-winner; developing an effective strategy almost certainly does.

The danger of not planning early is illustrated by the case of Mrs Gray. She telephoned me to say that her son, aged eleven, was in his last year at a state primary school in inner London and she did not know where he should go next. The available comprehensive schools were among the least successful academically in the whole country. She could afford independent day education, but her son stood no chance of passing the entrance exam. He had had a 'wonderful teacher' in his first two years at primary school, but then 'a series of complete duds'. Other parents in the same position had thought ahead and provided two or more years of extra tuition for their children. If only she had started planning her son's education sooner, she could have done the same. Now, having fallen so far behind academically, it was extremely unlikely that he would pass the entrance examination.

Mrs Gray's dilemma also illustrates that the key to developing a successful strategy is to identify as early as possible the best available secondary schools. You should then identify the most promising route into these schools, via the state primary schools or the independent preparatory schools; and, continuing to work backwards, the best nursery and pre-prep schools.

Planning your strategy this way round does not imply that education before the ages of eleven or thirteen is less important. But, by identifying the best secondary schools first, you are more likely to make the right choice for the early years.

There is another reason for basing your strategy on the secondary school. However good a child's early education, it is the secondary school that is the springboard to university and the adult world. A bad secondary school will squander the gains of the early years whereas a good one will develop the resources to go on learning and adapting in a changing world.

By 'the best available secondary schools' I mean the best for your children, and those that are within your reach both geographically and financially. That definition begs a number of questions which I have put in the form of a chart.

You may be tempted to refuse at the first hurdle. How can we know a child's educational needs at the age of three? Unless you are dealing with an infant prodigy or a child with a physical or mental handicap, you have to assume that each of your children will attend mainstream schools and that they are likely to remain in school or college to take A levels at seventeen or eighteen. That may not be what happens, but it is a mistake to start out with lower expectations.

What you will be able to afford at a given point in the future may also be difficult to assess. Remember that school fees are rising faster than inflation. As the market for boarding shrinks, some schools are trying to hold annual increases to inflation or below, but as they are likely to be schools in trouble, you would be opting for a cut-price ticket aboard a sinking ship. You should therefore be particularly wary of small boarding schools that offer sales gimmicks – such as a partial refund of fees if your child fails at A level or university entrance.

The same note of caution applies to scholarships given by schools and financial help given by the government; scholarships seldom cover more than half the cost of the fees and the government's assisted places scheme is being phased out. While not discounting the possibility of financial help, you should not build your whole strategy on the assumption that it will be available.

Whether or not you can afford independent education, you should check out the local state secondary schools. How do their academic records compare with those of the independent schools you are considering? What about their facilities, their

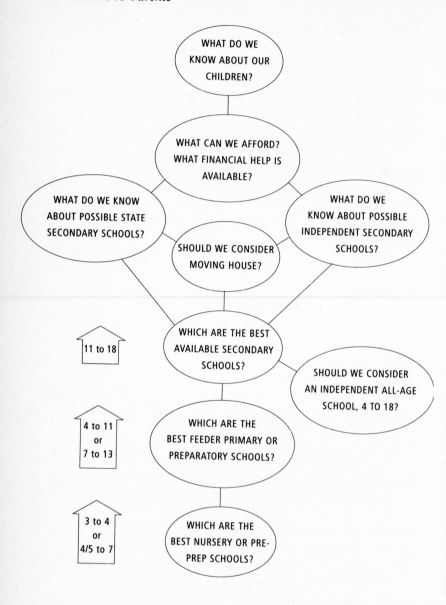

Figure 1: Strategy based on choice of secondary school

out of school activities and the values the school professes to uphold?

If you cannot afford independent education and the state schools within reach have a poor reputation, you may wish to consider moving house. For most parents this is not an option but for the Smiths it was. Their case illustrates both the advantages of moving house and the importance of having a strategy based on the best available secondary schools.

The Smiths lived in Brighton, East Sussex, and have a son and two daughters. Mr Smith worked in London – so, in theory, they could move anywhere within commuting distance. Their son and elder daughter, aged seven and four, had started at small local independent day schools, but the parents had no strategy and had given no serious thought to what should happen at the secondary stage. They spoke of keeping their options open.

When they did start to plan, they quickly realized that they would not be able to afford independent education for all three children. They also knew that they did not wish to treat their children differently, and that the local independent and state secondary schools had a poor record and reputation. So, if they were going to develop a successful strategy, they would have to target good state secondary schools somewhere else.

They chose Sevenoaks in Kent because it was within reach of good state secondary schools, both for boys and for girls. Then they checked on where the best feeder primary schools were and moved house accordingly. The children went from the good feeder primary school to the Judd School for Boys in Tonbridge and Tunbridge Wells School for Girls, two of the best state secondary schools in the country. The price the parents paid was a somewhat higher mortgage, but they obtained for their children a good education at no cost.

The key to their success was knowing *where* to move. They started with the A level league tables from which they picked out the most successful state schools for boys and for girls. Then they checked the local estate agents to find out what good local schools were doing to house prices. Combining a list of good schools and affordable housing gave them a choice of three areas from which they selected the one which suited them best.

The success of their strategy was also dependent upon the three children getting in to the schools of their choice. For parents targeting good state schools or good independent day schools, whether their children qualify for entry is the question on which the whole strategy rests.

You could live in London where the competition for good education is particularly fierce. In that situation there are many possible variations on the strategic theme, including sending your children out of London altogether to boarding school, but the essentials of a good strategy do not alter.

Identify the best available secondary schools and again work backwards. There are so few good state secondary schools in London that entry to them is as competitive as to the good independents. Identifying the best route into these schools can be difficult: popular state secondary schools are very reluctant to reveal where their successful applicants come from. They do not wish to expose bad primary schools, or make public how many of their own entry comes from independent schools. The government, which makes a virtue of giving parents information from schools, refuses to insist that information about entry to popular schools is made available. So you may have to make use of local intelligence – as the Smiths did.

If you want to use the state primary schools and then move your children to one of the independent day schools at eleven, you need to remember the case of Mrs Gray; they will almost certainly need two years of private tuition to give them a realistic chance in the entrance exams.

In London, and elsewhere, the independent sector offers a way of simplifying your strategy in the shape of all-age schools. These schools recruit as early as four and provide what they describe as 'a seamless education' to the age of eighteen. They are distinct from those independent schools such as Westminster and St Paul's which have their own preparatory school, but insist that all candidates for entry to the senior school at thirteen take the same competitive exam.

The number of all-age schools is increasing in response to parental demand and the schools need to scoop the pool of talent. The wisdom of subjecting your children to a competitive exam at the age of four and of their spending all their schooldays on the same campus is, however, hotly disputed. There are no all-age state schools except for children with special needs.

Of all the essentials of a successful strategy, the one parents are most likely to forget is the need to start *planning early*. Mrs Gray's son is now in his second year at a local comprehensive and, in his mother's words, 'he is falling behind his contemporaries in independent schools every day'. She cannot afford to send him out of London to board but she could have afforded to have given the extra tuition he needed to gain entry to one of London's independent day schools.

The Smiths did not start planning early either. Like so many parents they assumed that the secondary stage would look after itself, that the right way forward for their children at eleven or thirteen would somehow emerge from the mist like a landscape in the morning sun. When they did realize the danger they acted decisively to give their children a good education.

It is no good wishing we lived in a country where all this planning and manoeuvring to get our children into good schools was not necessary. That is dream land. There *is* first class education out there if you know how to get it. Be realistic, plan far ahead, be ruthless in pursuit of your children's interests, and make sure you have enough information on all the schools you are considering. The final choice is bound to be something of a leap of faith – but it does not have to be a leap in the dark.

Yours sincerely
John Rae

3 Will I have to pay fees to guarantee my son and daughter a good education?

Dear Juliet

The short answer is that it depends where you live. There are good state secondary schools in some parts of the country and where there are good secondary schools you can be pretty certain that there are good feeder primary schools, so that in all these areas the structure of good education exists for which you do not have to pay fees.

If you live in Buckinghamshire, for example, you could pay fees to send your son to Stowe, an independent school with fine buildings in a beautiful country setting but with a modest academic record; or you could send him free to one of the eight state schools that have consistently better academic results.

The phenomenon of the state school with a better academic record than the local independent school is not confined to the south of England, or to those counties, such as Buckinghamshire, that kept their selective grammar schools when others abolished selection and 'went comprehensive'.

However, it is not entirely fair to compare state day schools that select their pupils (even where the 11+ exam has officially been abolished) with independent boarding schools that can seldom afford to be choosy about their intake. There are fewer examples of state day schools with better academic records than the local independent day schools but they are interesting nevertheless. In Kingston-upon-Thames, the top local authority for public exam results, the two leading state schools,

Tiffin Girls School and Tiffin Boys School, have better academic records than the local independent day school, Kingston Grammar School. In Lancashire, the successful state schools such as the boys and girls grammar schools in Lancaster outperform all but the best independent day schools who are themselves among the best in the country.

There is more to education than academic results, but in some of these examples, the size of the academic lead suggests that in other ways too the schools that charge no fees are superior.

That is why I say that the short answer to your question is that it depends where you live. But while a good education is available free in some areas, the best education, certainly the best academic education, costs money. The top fifty schools in the A level league table all charge fees. Many schools in the bottom half of the league table also charge fees. So while you may have to pay fees for excellence, paying fees certainly does *not* guarantee a good education, a simple truth that many middle class parents continue to ignore.

You do not live within reach of a good state school and, if I understand your letter correctly, moving to another area is not a realistic proposition. But don't despair: the choice is not between paying nothing and paying boarding school fees that are not far short of your annual salary as a teacher. There are all sorts of combinations of fee paying and non-fee paying that parents use to get the best education that is available. Moving in and out of the independent sector is common practice nowadays; the important thing is to use whatever money you can afford at the right time and in the most effective way.

The first step is to check what help is available towards paying independent school fees. As a single parent on a modest salary your best bet would have been the assisted places scheme, but there is no way of knowing whether the scheme will be operating in nine years' time when your older child reaches secondary school age. Labour is committed to ending the scheme; the Conservatives are committed to restoring it.

While you cannot rely on the scheme being restored, you should not exclude it altogether from your calculations. Ignore the political arguments. All you should be concerned with is whether the scheme can help your children. The essential information about the outgoing scheme is as follows.

The scheme was started in 1981 and its aim was to open independent schools to 'children who are academically able and whose parents cannot afford the full tuition fees'. About 5700 places were available each year (though a Conservative government would have increased that total) in just under 300 independent schools. Most of the places were at the age of eleven, though there were some at five, thirteen and sixteen. Looking a long way ahead, you should not lose sight of assisted places in the sixth form at two of the best academic schools in the country – Winchester College for boys and St Swithun's School, Winchester, for girls – both of which are in travelling distance from your home for a sixteen-year-old.

The best summary of the scheme, which lists all schools taking part, is published by the Independent Schools Information Service. If the scheme is restored, I think you should ask yourself these questions. Is there a *good* independent school within daily travelling distance that offers assisted places at eleven? Are your children likely to be academically able enough to win places in a competitive field? Will you qualify for financial assistance and be able to make up the difference between the level of assistance and the full fee?

You should also bear in mind that just because a school offers assisted places it does not mean it is worth sending your children to. One of the curious aspects of the scheme – that even its critics do not seem to have noticed – is that although it is intended for the academically able, in some areas the independent schools offering assisted places are less good academically than the local state schools, so the taxpayer is funding a move that is not necessary.

The scheme embraces some of the best and some of the least

successful schools in the independent sector. In Hampshire, you have two of the best, Portsmouth High School for Girls and Portsmouth Grammar School which is mixed. If you are considering any others in the county that offer assisted places, you should look carefully at their academic record.

You cannot know at this stage whether your children will be academically able. My advice is to work on the assumption that they will be, and then consider how best to deploy your resources to increase their chances of winning an assisted place.

At least 60 per cent of assisted places at a school must be given to the pupils from state primary schools, so you do not have to pay fees up to eleven to give your children a sporting chance. If your resources are limited, money spent on good nursery education and on some private tuition when your children are at primary school level is probably the best course. But there are various combinations of paying and not paying that are possible in these early years and you will have to judge which is right in the light of your circumstances at the time and of the quality of the local primary schools. Financial help from any source other than the assisted places scheme when your children are under eleven is very difficult to obtain. Some independent preparatory schools do offer scholarships but they are rare and financial help for the under sevens is even rarer.

If your children *are* offered assisted places, you will still have to contribute to the fees unless your gross income before tax is less than £10,000 a year. Taking your present salary of about £15,000 a year as a yardstick, you would have to contribute about £1000 a year, which is about one quarter of the annual day fees at Portsmouth High School for Girls. You will need to do your own calculations nearer the time but it is unlikely that the proportion of the fees you will have to contribute will change – unless, of course, you become a head teacher and double your salary.

You will only receive help with extras, such as travel and uniform, if you had qualified for help when your children attended the local state school.

If the assisted places scheme exists, it will not provide your children with good academic education for free, but it will bring that education within your reach. The scholarships and bursaries offered by independent schools are seldom as generous as those provided by the assisted places scheme. A typical academic scholarship is worth half the fees, though wealthier schools may add a bursary to further reduce expenses should the half fees still seem too high to attract a bright boy or girl whose parents have a low income.

The key to understanding the independent schools' approach to scholarships is to recognize that the schools are motivated by self-interest not charity. When politicians threaten to remove the school's charitable status, the schools protest that they are spending vast sums on scholarships and bursaries for the poor and needy. That is not really the true picture. About 18 per cent of pupils in independent schools are given financial help by the schools themselves. Most of these are bright boys and girls from middle class homes. This is particularly true of schools which recruit at thirteen where the scholarships are, in practice, only open to middle-class families who can afford an expensive preparatory school.

During my sixteen years as headmaster of Westminster, only one of the ten annual Queen's Scholarships – that is to say one out of one hundred and sixty – was awarded to a candidate from a state school, and in his case his parents had paid for private tuition to prepare him for the examination.

Eton has at least recognized this problem and now offers four junior scholarships a year to boys at state primary schools. The winners spend two or three years at a preparatory school, at Eton's expense, and are then guaranteed a place at Eton at thirteen, with full fees paid if necessary.

Independent day schools that recruit at eleven do draw on the state primary schools but, with a few exceptions, they have limited funds for scholarships: hence their enthusiasm for the assisted places scheme.

Scholarships at independent schools are for recruiting talent, not for dispensing charity. If you think your financial circumstances will increase your children's chances of being awarded scholarships, you will be mistaken. The schools need academic talent to maintain their prominent position in the academic league table, and they are prepared to pay for it. They are also prepared to pay for musical talent, artistic talent and – a recent innovation – sporting talent.

From the schools' point of view this approach makes sense. They operate in a highly competitive environment where success in various fields catches the eye of prospective customers. From your point of view, the scholarships are less interesting than the assisted places scheme. There is no need to rule them out altogether, but I would not build your strategy around the hope of your children winning scholarships, however talented they may turn out to be.

The bursaries that some independent schools offer *are* based on parental need, but the schools tend to use them to top up scholarships or to tide over promising pupils whose parents have fallen on hard times. Bursaries are seldom generous and you should not bank on getting help in this way. Nor should you bank on receiving help with independent school fees from the local education authority. It would be worth checking what their criteria for helping is, but do not be disappointed if you are given a dusty answer. Most local authorities are very reluctant to admit that their own schools cannot provide for every educational need. With charitable trusts, I do not think it is even worth checking; if they give any help at all with school fees, it is in an emergency such as the father's death when the child is half way through an independent school education.

This may sound negative, but I am anxious that you should not spend too much time considering unrealistic options. Some parents persist in believing that their child will go to an independent school when it is clear that they will never be able to pay the fees. Each autumn, several children start their first term at independent schools with new uniforms and high hopes, only to be withdrawn after a few weeks when the schools discover that the parents have been bluffing or living in a world of fantasy. Perhaps the parents imagine the school will take pity on the child and waive the fees, but schools never do.

There is one final option you might like to consider, even though you say you do not want your children to go to boarding school. Though most of the leading boarding schools have long ago abandoned any pretence that they are offering opportunity to the children of the poor, a few of these schools have tried to remain true to that part of their foundation. The best and the best known of these schools is Christ's Hospital.

Christ's Hospital is an extraordinary phenomenon. It is an independent, boarding school for boys and girls aged eleven to eighteen, founded in 1552 to educate London's poor and now situated in West Sussex. It has the best A level results in that part of the country and all the out-of-school activities you would expect to find in a good school. Yet its tradition and admissions policy is to give preference to the children of parents who cannot pay independent school fees. Of the 800 boys and girls in the school, 300 pay no fees at all and only 2 per cent pay full fees. The average fee paid (in 1997) is £1700 a year, which is within your range, and the average parental income is £16,000, which is exactly your income.

I realize that your first choice is likely to be a day school for both your children, but don't leave Christ's Hospital out of your calculations. There is no hurry. You cannot register your children for that school until their ninth birthday. Three quarters of Christ's Hospital's intake comes from state primary schools so you would not have to spend money on school fees in the early years.

I do hope these thoughts are helpful.

Yours sincerely
John Rae

4 Does it matter still in Britain where you were at school?

Dear Tim and Jenny

It matters less and less and in most walks of life it doesn't matter at all. What *does* matter is that Peter should be educated at a good school, because that *will* give him the edge – but whether it is a famous public school or an unknown state school will be of no interest to most people he meets or to his future employers. That archetypal English question designed to put people in their place – 'Where were you at school?' – is seldom asked nowadays, except by an older generation who have failed to notice that times have changed.

Some people have been slow to recognize that the change has occurred. They insist that the only reason they did not get a particular job or promotion is that they did not go to the right school. Others argue more persuasively that the link between the leading public schools and the most influential jobs is so long established that it is inconceivable that it has disappeared altogether. 'In England, whom you know has always been more important than what you know,' writes the historian Robert Skidelsky. 'The country is still run by the old boy network'.

This perception is wholly understandable. For generations, pupils coming from the top public schools cast a spell over the job market, so that employers were almost literally enthralled; if you had been to what was supposedly an inferior school, you believed that many of the more prestigious jobs were immediately closed to you. People were kept in their place not so much by open discrimination as by a sort of hypnosis that imposed low expectations. The exceptions, who reached positions of power from humble origins, only served to prove the rule. Until the second half of this century, perhaps until even later, Britain was a society in which class mattered and the school you attended helped to define your class.

It is this spell that has been broken. It may linger in the popular imagination, but today the exceptions are those who are able to use the connections they made at school to advance their careers. Etonians may still give each other jobs in some sectors of the City, and I imagine it is still difficult to obtain a commission in the Life Guards unless you have been to one of the grander schools. But who cares? For most independent school pupils, the old school tie opens no doors. Like everybody else, they have to rely on their own ability and qualifications.

Data from the National Child Development Study, which has followed the fate of 11,000 children born in the same week in 1958, suggests that ability is five times more important than private education in determining what sort of career those children are following in their thirties.

If you still have doubts, I think it is probably because the leading independent schools have adapted so successfully to the new situation. No wonder people think things have not changed when three of the top schools in the A level league tables – Winchester, Westminster and Eton – are the same three that were singled out by Parliament as being in a class of their own in the reign of Charles II.

But don't be misled. Whatever may have happened in the past, the pupils from leading independent schools now get ahead on merit. They have dumped class snobbery and easy entry for the sons of former pupils as ruthlessly as they dispose of unsuccessful headmasters, and have embraced merit in the form of academic excellence. If their pupils have an advantage, it is because they are at good schools – not because they are at public schools.

An editorial in a recent issue of the *Independent Schools Bulletin* opened with the sentence: 'The watchword of the independent schools is the pursuit of excellence'. I take a more cynical view. The watchword of these resilient independent schools is the pursuit of *power*. If you track the careers of public school pupils over the centuries, you will see that the emphasis shifts perpetually to wherever power lies within society. When bishops had real influence, almost every bishopric was filled by a former pupil of a leading public school; now that bishops matter less, a bishop from a leading public school is hard to find. The schools have embraced academic excellence because it is the new route to power, not just because it helps to guarantee their survival.

Peter may never be interested in exercising power whether as a politician or behind the scenes, but the chances are that he will be interested in a good job and here, too, the route to success is via academic achievement. The route leads from a good school – whether independent or state does not matter – to the top universities, particularly Oxford and Cambridge. That is where the top firms recruit and where the best career contacts are made. The best careers are not necessarily the highest paid, but they offer status, job satisfaction, influence and, at the very least, a comfortable lifestyle.

I cannot emphasize too strongly that success on this route into adulthood does not depend on where you were at school, but on academic achievement. Skidelsky is wrong. In Britain today, what you know is more important than whom you know or where you learnt it.

Given the tenacity with which this country clings to the past, I suppose we should be cautious about saying that merit has finally triumphed over class. But of one thing I am sure – the tide of school snobbery has gone out.

The success of girls' independent schools at GCSE and at A level is at least partly because these schools have never been able to assure their pupils that the old school tie would be an adequate substitute for academic qualifications. The pioneers of girls' education embraced academic excellence from the start. Parents did not send their daughters to the great Victorian foundations, such as Cheltenham Ladies College and the North London Collegiate School, in order to make contacts which would be useful in later life. This emphasis on academic achievement is paying dividends as girls increasingly set the pace in the race for the best universities and the best jobs.

Competition for places at the best universities is fiercer for both sexes than it has ever been. The expansion of the university sector to include former polytechnics has persuaded many sixth formers that a university degree is not worth having unless it is from one of the top institutions. Do pupils from the leading independent schools have an advantage here? At first sight, it appears that they do. Independent schools educate only 7.5 per cent of the school population, yet consistently win about 45 per cent of the places at Oxford and Cambridge. But entry to Oxford and Cambridge is based on A level grades, and the top fifty places in the A level league table are occupied by independent schools. The striking thing is not that the pupils from these schools win 45 per cent of the entry to Oxford and Cambridge, but that they do not win a larger share. They have an advantage, but it is based on merit not family connections.

Whether some colleges are biased *against* candidates from the leading independent schools is impossible to say, but you might conclude that if Peter wanted to go to Oxford or Cambridge he would be at no disadvantage if he applied from one of the academically strong state schools. Oxford and Cambridge are keen to increase the proportion of successful applicants from state schools, so if the applicant's school has any bearing on the decision nowadays it is more likely to work in favour of state school applicants.

It will be many years before Peter has to worry about university application; in that time the relative merits of different universities may change, though it is unlikely that Oxford and Cambridge will lose their pre-eminent position. If your question had been, 'Does it still matter in Britain where you were at university?', I would have answered 'yes' without hesitation.

In the USA no one asks where you were at school, but the standing of your university has a direct impact on your career prospects. As Britain moves nearer to that position it is even more important to send your child to a good school; one that will facilitate access to a good university, rather than a brand name with a modest academic record. By all means spend money on a good independent school for Peter, if no good state school is within range, but don't waste money buying him an old school tie.

Yours sincerely
John Rae

5 Do our children have to be part of the academic rat race?

Dear Dr and Mrs Attwood

All this talk of A level grades and league tables is bound to make some parents more determined than ever to protect their children from what they see as the downside of promoting academic success: too much pressure on the child, and too little time for all the other things that matter in education and growing up.

Many teachers, too, are worried that schools are becoming mere production lines, churning out test scores and exam grades, not well-rounded young people. A teacher, who has retired early from one of the most academically successful independent schools, told me he could no longer bear to see the narrowing of the pupils' horizons – the way the boys and girls have no interest in anything except what they need to pass exams.

Even if his disenchantment leads him to overstate the case, what this man has to say would draw spontaneous applause from a gathering of teachers. The perception is that schools are in danger of sacrificing true education for the sake of a better place in the academic league tables.

It is this perception that I quarrel with. Academic competition has its casualties, but so does lack of competition. There is no single method of educating children that does not leave some of them disheartened, and I suspect that possibly more pupils are disheartened as a result of being protected from competition than by being exposed to it. So that when you say that you do not want your children to be part of the academic rat race, do not imagine that your policy will shield them from disappointment. It might, however, deny them the stimulus they need. A slower pace with less academic pressure may suit them; if it does, and you can find a good school that is consciously setting out to provide this (as distinct from a bad school that just has low expectations), you will have chosen well. But you should not assume that your children will share your dislike of the competitive ethos in education.

Some children thrive on competition from a young age, while others are so lacking in self-confidence they will not risk giving an answer for fear of appearing foolish. One of our grand-daughters, who is seven, is obsessed with winning, so much so that on our Sunday visits I am hard pushed to find ways to ensure she loses occasionally. She is a bad loser and needs practice. It would be madness for her parents to keep her out of what you call the academic rat race. She is a competitive animal. I doubt whether there is anything more competitive than a seven-year-old girl who wants to win. When I read that in the workplace the men tend to be more competitive while the women try to build a consensus, I think of Francesca.

Her younger brother wants to win, too, but seldom does. It is not the competitive instinct he lacks, but his sister's single-minded determination to concentrate her forces where it matters. She is the Napoleon of childhood games. His talents are scattered over the hills and are easily defeated because he has not learnt to co-ordinate them. To expose him to a competitive academic school, even if he could win a place, would probably be a disaster. Instead, he needs time and encouragement to bring his abilities under some form of control. The problem for his parents is not whether to opt out of the academic rat race, but where to find the right alternative. Schools that really do cater for the less competitive child, who needs learning support, are to be found almost exclusively in the independent boarding sector.

I do not know your children and they are too young perhaps for you to know whether or not they will thrive on competition. It would be a mistake to rule out a competitive academic education at this stage, but it would be a good time to ask yourselves what it is about academic competition you fear.

I know that the pressure on children can be so intolerable that some young people may feel driven to take their own lives when their exam results are disappointing. Any adolescent suicide is especially tragic because it seems so unnecessary – a wild exaggeration, but as a witness in the case against academic pressure it should be treated with caution. The number of adolescent suicides in which the worry about academic pressure or exam results appears to have been a major factor is very small. An analysis of suicidal teenagers' calls to Childline in 1994 shows that school and exam pressures account for only 1 per cent. This low figure cannot be explained by the reluctance of pupils in academic schools to seek help; Childline has calls from pupils in independent schools and selective state schools, mostly about bullying. All adolescents are vulnerable as they cross the bridge between childhood and adulthood, but that does not mean that they lack the necessary resilience to cope with disappointment.

What fools we make of ourselves when we try to protect our children from competition. In the late sixties, we abolished prizes, and even tried to disguise the fact that the division of forms was based on ability. Instead of calling the forms Lower Five A, B, C and so on, we gave them letters at random. We deceived no one, least of all the pupils. At other schools streaming by ability was abandoned altogether and researchers reported that all children did better in mixed ability groups. Educational research – what crimes are committed in thy name!

It is strange that as experienced teachers we refused to accept what as parents we knew perfectly well: you cannot shield your children from competition, but you can and must help them to learn how to handle the disappointments as well as the triumphs. Looking back, I am sure one of the reasons we rejected competition in the schools was that we had lost confidence in our ability to do just that. It was not competition that was found wanting, but our willingness to help pupils deal with it. Was there an element of laziness too? Helping pupils come to terms with failure takes much more time than allowing them to believe it does not exist.

Children can learn to handle competition as long as we do not leave them to cope alone. But they do not find it easy to handle parents who insist on entering the competition themselves, parents who worry too much or push too hard. I wish I could give you a formula for avoiding these damaging side effects of competition, but it is largely a matter of trial and error: of developing a feel for when your children do want to be asked how they got on at school and when they do not, of knowing when to tackle the teacher and when to leave well alone, of being able to distinguish between high expectations and unrealistic ambitions.

Your fear that academic competition makes people 'thoroughly selfish' echoes the attitude of Victorian schoolmasters who banned individual sports and encouraged team games. One understands the theory, but in practice there is no evidence that competitive people are more or less selfish than their less competitive peers.

Academic competition brings out the best in some children and it is a necessary part of education for all children. Whether its effect is good or bad depends on whether we, as parents and teachers, keep the whole business of exams, marks and orders in the correct perspective.

Making schools compete for the prestige of a higher place in the academic league tables may make them more inclined to lose a sense of perspective, but from the point of view of most pupils and their parents, that danger is far outweighed by the benefits. The principal result of the recent emphasis on academic competition is that pupils work harder, teachers are more professional and schools are better run; and this is true of independent as well as state schools.

There are few people outside the schools' world who realize how bad some of the teaching was in independent schools before academic results began to be taken seriously; how many lessons were taught off the cuff by teachers who did not know their subject, how much written work was never properly marked and how many red herrings masqueraded as a broad education.

If you were able to study the A level results of independent schools in the sixties, you would find that an astonishing number of pupils scored low grades, or failed to achieve any pass grades at all. That was not because they were less able than their successors of the nineties, but because teaching for exams was regarded as in some way beneath the dignity of the institution. Few parents complained. Most paid up, thanked the school for all it had done and then paid again for a year at a tutorial college – at the end of which their sons and daughters obtained the good A levels they should have got in the first place.

In the seventies, the leading independent schools woke up to the danger of taking such a *laissez-faire* attitude to public exams, but many other independent schools did little to improve the efficiency of their operation. Many state schools were equally opposed to teaching for exams, not because it was beneath their dignity but because they were ideologically opposed to competition. The truth is that for many state and independent schools and their teachers the national publicity given to academic league tables in the nineties came as a much-needed shot in the arm.

It is easy to overlook this unpalatable truth when the educational debate is centred on cuts in school budgets, particularly as they affect the size of classes. But, when schools had more money they were no more efficient. Ample resources without the stimulus of competition do not create good schools.

The teacher who retired early in despair at the narrowing of his pupils' horizons thought he saw a world disappearing; a world in which gifted teachers had the freedom to inspire their pupils with a disinterested love of learning. I question whether that world ever existed. There *were* gifted teachers, and those of us who encountered them know how lucky we were, but they were outnumbered by the lazy and incompetent – as I am sure you will remember. The new world may leave less time for scholarly discourse, but it gives the pupils as a whole a much better deal.

I think academic competition has helped to ensure that schools provide a better service, but I recognize that there are risks entailed. Encouraging competition between schools has always presented the headmaster or headmistress with the temptation to sacrifice the individual for the sake of the school's reputation. The publication of academic league tables has served to increase that temptation.

Even before league tables some independent schools, particularly urban day schools, were notorious for refusing to allow pupils to start on an A level course unless they were certain to pass. Schools set their own qualification for entry to the sixth form (in terms of O level, or since they were disbanded, GCSE passes), and as competition between schools increased, the qualifying standard was raised accordingly.

When top grades matter so much to the school's position in the league table, it is tempting to exclude any pupils who seem unlikely to achieve good grades. Heads who yield to that temptation, however, have crossed the line between setting a realistic qualification and 'academic cleansing'.

It is impossible to say how widespread 'academic cleansing' is. I do not like it any more than you, but it is not a reason for condemning all competition between schools. Instead, I would advise you to ask the head what the school's policy is. If you find the question difficult to frame, why not quote the prospectus of a London tutorial college, Davies, Laing & Dick, which states categorically: 'On no account will any student be withdrawn from an exam simply because the result may damage our statistics'. No school worth sending your children to should hesitate to make the same declaration.

The aspect of competition which most lends itself to your concept of a rat race, however, is not what happens when the children are at school, but the hectic scramble to get them in. The fierce competition for places at the best state and independent day schools inspires in some parents a state of acute anxiety. Like passengers on the Titanic they know there are too few lifeboats, and they fear their children will sink without trace if good schools turn them away.

The hectic scramble is at its worst in London, though the characteristics of the Titanic lifeboat syndrome – extra coaching, mock exams, parental anxiety and parental guilt – will be familiar to parents in other conurbations, such as Manchester and Birmingham, where the contrast between the academic independent schools and the inner city comprehensives is at its most stark.

But while we may recoil from the idea of children competing for places, are we sure that in practice any harm is done? Where are the casualties? I imagine the unsuccessful candidates are happily competing in their second or third choice school, having swiftly recovered from disappointment unless their parents made a big thing of it. They are heading for a brighter future than would have been the case if their parents had decided from the start that they did not want their children to be part of the academic rat race.

Yours sincerely
John Rae

6 Should our political, social and religious convictions influence our choice of school?

Dear Penelope

I think you should concentrate on obtaining the best available education for Bronwyn. With the exception of a strong and overriding religious commitment, no conviction should be allowed to deflect you from that goal.

Take the question of 'buying privilege', which certainly seems to worry some parents. Whether or not to pay fees is not a political or a moral question. You should approach it in a purely pragmatic way. Can we afford it? Is it worth it? You may believe that our society would be more at ease with itself if all children went to the local state school, but that should have no bearing on your decisions about your own child's education. What you think would be best for the country and what you think would be best for Bronwyn should be kept entirely separate.

Writing in the *Independent* in 1995 a teacher at an inner-city comprehensive agonized over what to do with her own child: 'I dare not go and look at private schools at all, lest I waver from my deeply-held principles that our British system is divisive and the root of many of the evils in our society'. However sincere, such an attitude confuses the parent's convictions with the individual needs of the child. The latter must take precedence.

The days when socialists sent their children to the local comprehensive on principle and middle-class boys were put down for their father's school at birth are over. This is the age of the single-minded consumer and the best buy. That may sound glib, but it is only another way of saying that, for today's parents, sentimental and ideological baggage has no place in the choice of their child's school.

Twenty years ago, Labour MPs were moving their children from independent to state schools to prove their socialist credentials. Today, they are more likely to choose the school they really want – independent or otherwise – and like Tony Blair and Harriet Harman, to defy any criticism levelled at them. One of the leading Labour MPs, Paul Boateng, expresses by his own actions the new parental approach – free from social engineering and political correctness:

> You have as a parent to choose for your children on the basis of what's best for those children. I've got five children; three of them are in the state sector, two of them are in the independent sector. You choose on the basis of what is good for your child, not on the basis of dogma or ideology . . .

This attitude makes a refreshing change from those middle-class parents who say they have moved their children out of the state schools 'very reluctantly', and 'with a heavy heart'.

The fact that many parents have no effective choice should have no bearing on your decision either. The fate of other children may concern you as a citizen; it should not concern you as a parent.

I know that part of you will find what I am saying unpalatable. You hold ideals about equal opportunity which I once held, but have compromised too often to lay claim to now. But your ideals are not compromised if, as Bronwyn's mother, you put what is best for her above all other considerations.

Nor should you feel guilty if one of your reasons for opting out of the local state school is that you do not want Bronwyn to mix with the other children who go there. Wanting your children to grow up with children from similar backgrounds is natural. The values you are teaching Bronwyn at home will be tested in the rough-and-tumble of any school she attends; there is no need to make the test more difficult than you have to. Some people wrongly regard such an attitude as snobbery. But the same desire to nurture the values that I care for would dissuade me from exposing my children to the rampant materialism of a 'gin-and-jag belt' boarding school.

I am puzzled, too, when parents say they want their children to go to a school with a social and ethnic mix. If it is a really good school, the mix may be regarded as a bonus. There are some outstandingly good schools which draw their pupils from across the social spectrum, such as King Edward's, Birmingham, among day schools, and Christ's Hospital in West Sussex, among boarding schools, but they are few and far between. Choosing a school on the grounds that it has a social and ethnic mix is a case of parents allowing their own social convictions to get in the way of their children's education.

Other social convictions about education can also often turn out to be prejudices. It can be genuinely difficult for parents to disentangle what they believe is best for their children from what they think would have been best for themselves, if only they could have their childhood all over again. Attitudes to co-education and boarding are good illustrations of this. Some parents insist that their children should go to co-educational or day schools, but when you ask them why, you discover that it is their own unhappy school-days that they are using as deciding factors.

Religious convictions, however, are very different. I am not talking about a vague feeling that Church of England schools may have better discipline. Strongly-held religious convictions, whether Christian, Moslem or Jewish, are convictions that see no distinction between religion and education. A Roman Catholic school is not a secular school with Roman Catholic overtones; to a greater or lesser degree every aspect of the school's life is informed by the faith.

When a Jesuit school says it 'is founded on the vision of

St Ignatius as expressed in his *Spiritual Exercises* and as practised and interpreted through the Jesuit system of education
begun in 1548', it means what it says. I remember looking at
the list of former pupils of another Jesuit independent school,
at Stonyhurst in Lancashire, and counting fifteen who had been
martyred for their faith. If parents share the strong religious
convictions of these schools they should not allow any other
considerations, not even academic standards, to take precedence. But if by religious convictions you mean a preference
for a school with Christian overtones, there are plenty of Anglican foundations to choose from so you will not need to make
religion the primary factor in your choice. Choose the best
school for Bronwyn, and ask about the school's religious life
afterwards.

It is not unusual for mother and father to hold different,
even strongly opposed, views about their children's education.
If the disagreement is because only one partner has strong
religious convictions, I cannot help. By their nature such convictions are not open to compromise. But if the disagreement
stems – as it so often does – from what are thought to be
political and social convictions, then the approach I recommend may help. To pay or not to pay, boarding or day,
co-ed or single sex, middle class or social mix – these are not
unimportant questions, but parents should try to resolve them
purely and simply with reference to their children's interests.
By not confusing children's interests with parents' convictions
– the mistake that inner-city teacher was making – any disagreement can be restricted to practical matters, thereby avoiding the empty rhetoric of political and social theory. Which
school would suit the children best? Which school would bring
out the best in them? Argue about these by all means, but
don't waste time arguing about whether Bronwyn would
benefit from being educated with children of different backgrounds and different ethnic groups.

In my experience, it is the father who is more likely to have
preconceived ideas and who needs more persuading that his

assumptions about the relative merits of different types of school are out of date. It is just as well, perhaps, that in more and more families it is the mother who takes the lead in the debate about the children's education and who is the contact between home and school. This is a far cry from *Tom Brown's Schooldays* when Squire Brown simply informed his wife one morning, 'I have arranged that Tom shall go to Rugby at once'.

No father would get away with that today. The mother's increasingly powerful voice in her children's education may be, like the unravelling of the old gender division of labour, just another step towards 'household equality'. Whatever the explanation, I think mothers are more likely than fathers to put the interests of their child before all other considerations. So, my advice is to follow your instincts and forget your ideals. Patronizing, cynical and sexist though that may sound, I still think it is the right advice.

Yours sincerely
John Rae

7 Are we going to be consumers or partners in our children's education?

Dear Siobhan

I hope you are going to be both, though combining the two roles is not easy. Partnership implies co-operation with the school, but there will be times when you are dissatisfied with the school's performance and feel less inclined to co-operate than to demand an improvement in the service. As a partner, you understand that a new teacher takes time to settle down; as a consumer, you may want your child moved straightaway to a more experienced teacher's class.

The tension between the partner and the consumer will be ever-present, so it is as well to start out on the long journey through your children's education with a realistic awareness of the possibilities and limitations of both roles.

Parents' ambivalence towards their children's school is nothing new. What is new is that a relationship which no one thought worth taking seriously has acquired a rhetoric of its own and a key position on the education agenda. Ambivalence is now defined in terms of 'partnership' and 'consumerism'.

Does that mean that there has been a real change in the relationship between home and school? The way the relationship operates *has* changed, but whether the age-old wariness on the side of the school has been modified, I am less sure. Fear of parental interference remains, I suspect, part of every teacher's psychological profile.

It needs no research to reveal that your children will do

better at school if you show an interest in their work, but partnership suggests a more active involvement in your children's education, even in the day-to-day life of the school. It is this crossover from interest to active involvement which is a recent development.

In the state schools, partnership has been something of a shotgun marriage. Parents have been making overtures since the 1880s when the Parents' National Educational Union was formed, but it was not until the 1980s that Parliament forced the schools to accept the parents as partners. The Education Acts of 1986 and 1988 increased the number of parent governors and gave parents the right to question governors about the management of the school at an annual meeting. These Acts also gave all governors the right to have a say in the day-to-day running of the school.

These measures had more to do with political ideology than belief in partnership. Politicians, who were frustrated by their inability to improve standards in schools, decided to use parents as a means of putting pressure on teachers. In the jargon of the time, power in education was to be taken away from the 'producers' and given to the 'consumers'.

I mention the history so that if you find the teachers uneasy about some of the implications of partnership, you will know the reason. Making the best of a shotgun marriage is not the same as being enthusiastic about it. The existence of formal structures, such as Parent Teacher Associations, does not always help. Although some heads work happily with the PTA, I can sympathize with the teachers' unease, particularly when a senior official of the National Confederation of Parent Teacher Associations suggests that teachers' contracts should stipulate that 'ignoring parents will result in dismissal'. I would have thought that there were times when it was the teacher's duty to ignore the parents in the interests of the child.

You may think that teachers are over sensitive to parental criticism. I know that *I* did not find it easy to keep calm when told that a parent had been critical of my performance as a teacher or as a headmaster; I took it personally, not professionally as I should have done. Yet, teachers *do* take criticism personally; they are more insecure, despite their outward show of authority, than any group of people I have come across. I am not suggesting you should ignore their faults, only that they may need more encouragement than you might expect when you read about partnership in the school prospectus.

Partnership is most likely to work well in infant and primary schools. It does not work so well when children move up to secondary school. If you are closely involved with your children's schools up to the age of eleven, be prepared for a change in the style of partnership which may leave you feeling out of touch. The same is true in the independent sector where parents identify with the life of the preparatory school, but find it difficult to have such a close relationship with the senior school.

Senior schools are larger and less inclined to involve parents. Your children, too, will be less communicative as they encounter adolescence; they do not want you to have too close a relationship with the school. If you try to continue the close relationship you had with the school when your children were young, I'm afraid you may find you are rebuffed by both your children and the school.

The close relationship you can forge in the early years is anyway the one that matters. It is also the easiest to establish. Teachers in infant schools embrace partnership with enthusiasm; little or no trace of a shotgun marriage here. Before your child starts, the school will send you information about how the school works and a pre-reception booklet with ideas and activities for you and your child to share – aimed at making it easier for your child to adapt to the school environment. There will also be advice about what you can do to help your child settle down when the 'big' day arrives, and about how to avoid misunderstandings between school and home. 'The beginning of school is a milestone in every child's life – and every parent's life, too,' writes the head of a Kent infants' school to new parents. 'For your own peace of mind and your children's happiness use every opportunity to make good relationships and build bridges between home and school. While your child is finding his or her feet, you can help by keeping the pressure down at home. And get your patience, tolerance and sense of humour into good shape now – you'll be needing them.'

In the infants' and primary schools there is one particular form of partnership which you will find teachers enthusiastic about, and that is help from parents in teaching their children to read. When classes are large, partnership is a way of recruiting parents as auxiliary teachers. It also makes sense and you will find that the school gives you guidance on exactly what sort of help is needed. As the children grow older, the range of subjects being studied makes it more difficult for parents to help, but you should not worry about that. Parents are not expected to be experts and it is good for your children to discover that they know more than you do. I can think of few things more likely to undermine a young person's confidence than a parent who knows all the answers.

Whether or not you wish to become more closely involved with the school as a parent governor is for you to decide. There is one thing about governors, however, you should check. The head should be the chief executive, but the education acts have created a situation where governors can, and in some cases do, usurp the head's authority. A key question to ask the head is who has the final say in the appointment of teaching staff; if the governors can overrule the head, one of the essential characteristics of a good school – that the head chooses his own staff – will be missing.

If your children go to state schools, your statutory rights on matters such as parent governors are published by the government as a Parents' Charter. It is a useful *aide-mémoire* of what you can expect from the school by way of reporting on your child's progress and what the school will expect of you by way of support for its policies on homework and behaviour.

But in one respect it is a misleading document. It states that, 'You have a right to a good education for your child'. You do not need me to tell you that these words are worthless and that if you want a good education for your child in contemporary Britain, you will have to fight for it every inch of the way.

Partnership between parents and schools in the independent sector is a marriage of convenience. All independent schools have responded to the national mood in favour of more openness to parents, but the real impetus for change has been the shrinking boarding market. The leading independent day schools for boys and girls have more applicants than they need; they do what is expected of them by way of parents' meetings, but you may find their attitude to parents is high-handed, even arrogant. It is a seller's market. 'Do you have any favourite pupils?' a parent asked Dr Eric James, High Master of Manchester Grammar School in the 1950s. 'Yes, madam,' was the reply, 'orphans.' Forty years on, the belief that parents should be seen occasionally but not heard is not far below the surface of some independent day schools.

Independent boarding schools can no longer afford to treat parents like embarrassing relatives who have to be invited to family functions, but who should otherwise be kept at arm's length. With very few exceptions they are short of pupils. Offering partnership to prospective parents is one way of attracting business.

The prospectuses make it sound as though a revolution in attitudes has occurred. 'Co-operation between parents and teachers is essential,' says one; 'We encourage informal contacts and there is a Parents Committee which meets each term to discuss matters of common interest with the Headmaster, the staff and a member of the Board of Governors.'

The unwelcoming facade that made parents feel like intruders has been replaced by the spirit of glasnost: 'We want parents to feel welcome at Clayesmore on every occasion, and hope they will feel fully involved and consulted throughout their son's or daughter's education.'

Geographical remoteness is also no bar to partnership. The headmaster of Ampleforth, a Roman Catholic boarding school on the edge of the North Yorkshire Moors, holds regular meetings throughout the country 'to consult and inform parents on major issues'.

From your point of view, it is important to discover exactly what form of partnership the schools are offering. They are not offering parent power: if there are parents who are governors in independent schools, it is by chance, seldom by design. 'Inform and consult' does not mean that parents have a role in deciding school policy. What is on offer is a much greater willingness than in the past to communicate with parents face to face and not just through end-of-term reports; to discuss with parents non-academic issues, such as illegal drugs, on which the school needs the parents' help, and to encourage parents to feel part of the wider school community.

That is probably as far as most parents with children at independent schools want partnership to go. The majority show little enthusiasm for Parent Teacher Associations, which is just as well because such formal structures are anathema to most independent school heads.

If I was a parent again with children in independent schools, I would expect to be consulted about their choice of GCSE and A level subjects, and to be kept informed of their academic progress via a combination of termly reports and an annual meeting with their teachers. I would expect the housemaster or housemistress to let me know from time to time how our children were developing as people and coping with adolescence, but I would not expect to be told every time they put a foot wrong.

As far as the day-to-day running of the school is concerned, I would be happy to leave that to the head and the staff, but I would want to have the opportunity to express a view should a major change in school policy be contemplated. I would not want to vote in a parents' referendum. Parents, like pupils, have a short-term interest in the school; decisions that affect the long term should be made by the head and the governing body.

Everybody pays for their children's education one way or another, so in that sense you will be a consumer as well as a partner. If teachers are uneasy about some aspects of partnership, then they positively dislike the idea of parents as consumers. You may think their sensitivities are rather precious, but remember that for many teachers their choice of career was a deliberate rejection of the commercial world. That is why the language of the market-place is so unwelcome to them.

On the other hand, teachers should not be allowed to get away with low standards just because their performance cannot be measured in terms of profit and loss. They are accountable to you as parents, as well as to the government and to society at large. The teachers who teach your children are not doing you a favour; they are paid to do a job and you should expect value for money, whether you are paying directly through fees or indirectly through taxation.

You have a difficult balance to strike, all the more so because you are afraid that if you complain too much your child may suffer. My advice is to try to develop the sort of relationship with the school which enables frank things to be said on either side for the sake of your child. I do not pretend that will be easy, but when you are considering a school you might ask the head whether he or she thinks an open and honest relationship between school and parents is possible.

You are a consumer with rights, but you are also a parent with responsibilities. The head has the right to expect that you will instil good discipline at home, just as much as you have the right to expect the head to create an ethos of good discipline at school. Your roles as partner and consumer may sometimes be hard to reconcile, but they are also interdependent. You will not get good value as a consumer if you fail to accept your responsibilities as a partner.

The emphasis on parents' rights is bound to elicit a corresponding emphasis on parents' responsibilities. Both the government and the opposition have already proposed a home-school contract to cover such topics as responsibility to see that children do their homework. Many North American independent schools go further and require parents to sign a statement agreeing 'to abide by the rules, regulations and policies' of the school. Some American schools also stipulate that parents attend parent-teacher meetings twice a year and this idea too is being discussed in Britain.

I expect the trend towards more binding agreements between home and school to gather momentum in this country – and not just as a reaction to parents' rights. Over time schools have been asked to take on responsibility for wider aspects of the upbringing of children, and teachers believe, with justification, that some parents are abandoning a task which they find either difficult or inconvenient. A desire to make such parents keep their side of the bargain is therefore understandable.

Whatever happens, do not encourage your children to see themselves as consumers. The relationship – one might say the balance of power – between teachers and pupils has shifted in favour of the latter. This is partly the teachers' own fault; in the 1960s and 1970s, they gave away some of their traditional authority in exchange for what they thought would be better relations with the pupils, only to find that mateyness was not what the pupils wanted. It is also partly the result of the 1989 Children Act which, while ensuring that schools were vigilant in protecting children from abuse, made even young children aware of their power to threaten teachers with a frivolous or malicious accusation.

To this shift of power, the idea of the pupil as a consumer has given added impetus. When state secondary schools are competing for pupils, they are tempted to treat primary school pupils (not just their parents) as consumers. Open days at the local comprehensive school become elaborate public relations exercises, in which the primary school pupils are given gift packs and assured that this is a fun school where little will be demanded of them but the pursuit of happiness. Independent boarding schools anxious to fill empty beds are also giving more prominence in their prospectuses to the happiness, friendliness and fun that are on offer.

You see the danger. No one would wish children to be unhappy at school, but if they are wooed as consumers and get it into their heads that school life is going to be happy and learning is going to be fun, they will soon be disappointed. Worse still, if they start to *think* like consumers, they will discover too late that good academic results are not theirs by right.

Whichever strategy you adopt for your children's education, your relationship with their schools will be an important factor in the strategy's success. As with any other relationship, you will have to work at it. Headteachers are better at making promises than carrying them out, so despite what it may say in the prospectus, the nature of the relationship will largely depend on you. You will have to judge when to be a consumer and how to play your role as a partner.

Yours sincerely,
John Rae

8 How important are the academic league tables?

Dear Dr and Mrs Watson

Academic league tables tell parents more than schools are willing to acknowledge. The heads of independent and state schools tried hard to prevent league tables being published and are still not reconciled to them. Some of the heads' criticisms are well founded, but the league tables are here to stay and are an important source of information for parents choosing a school.

For their part, the heads say that they are happy to give prospective parents the exam results of individual schools, but that ranking schools on the basis of results is misleading because it takes no account of the schools' standard of entry. But there is an element of hypocrisy here. Heads refused to show their own school's results to parents until government and public opinion forced them to do so. What heads dislike about league tables is that they enable parents to compare different schools; and such unfavourable comparisons are taken personally by most heads. Their criticism of league tables, though couched in disinterested terms, partly reflects their desire to protect their own and their school's reputation. It is not the misleading nature of the league tables which worries them so much as the publication of clear evidence that some schools and some heads are better than others.

The heads are right to remind parents (if they needed reminding) that league tables take no account of the school's entry. The tables were never intended to show which schools do the most to improve their pupils' performances, and it is unlikely that such a 'value-added' table could be constructed, except perhaps for the two years between GCSE and A levels. So we have to make do with the raw data of the existing tables.

Two versions of the public exams taken by secondary school pupils are published each year: one in the late summer by the Independent Schools Information Service (ISIS) and one in November by the government's Department for Education and Employment. The ISIS version is used by the press to construct A level and GCSE league tables for independent schools and the academically successful state schools. The government's version is an analysis of *all* schools' and colleges' results in both exams, region by region, and is used by some newspapers to construct league tables of the 'top schools'.

The GCSE results are reported by the government as the proportion of the age group obtaining five or more GCSEs at grades A to C. It is a blunt measure that gives no credit to those who obtain the top grade, or the starred A grade available to the brightest pupils. The A level results are reported as the average point score based on an A grade being ten points, a B eight points and so on, a more sophisticated measure which does give credit to those who obtain the top grade.

This is one reason why the government's GCSE results are a less useful guide to a school's academic performance than the results of A level. The government's version of GCSE results may be said to be flawed in another way. At both GCSE and A level the government bases its calculations on the number of pupils in the age group, whereas ISIS includes all the pupils taking the exam that year, regardless of age. At A level this does not make much difference because the government's definition of the age group is so broad; but at GCSE where the definition is narrow – fifteen on the previous 31 August – the government's version of the results excludes bright pupils who take the exam early and overseas pupils who take the exam late. The results of independent boarding schools in particular can be between 10 per cent and 20 per cent lower in the government version than in the ISIS version.

Even if these limitations were not present, I would advise you not to put too much weight on GCSE results as a measure of a school's academic performance. Some schools take the exam more seriously than others: at Winchester, for example, many boys skip GCSE in some subjects because they are too easy, and the school prefers to concentrate on A level education. The A level results are a much better guide to a school's academic performance, though even here the two versions give parents different information.

The government version includes the result of A level General Studies, a paper that most academic independent schools regard as such a soft option that it should not be counted as an A level at all. But some schools, both independent and state, cynically use General Studies as a way to improve their A level average score.

The ISIS version of A level results excludes General Studies for this reason. I think it is right to do so, because too-easily-acquired top grades give a false impression of academic excellence. The inclusion of General Studies may lift a school twenty or more places in the A level ranking. But the precedent of excluding an exam which is regarded as too easy may have unforeseen consequences. Some subjects such as physics and mathematics are thought to be harder than others, such as history of art. Should a top grade in physics therefore be worth more than a top grade in history of art? Should history of art be excluded altogether?

The league tables based on the ISIS version of A level results are not perfect. They give an advantage to schools with a concentration of very bright pupils – for example, Winchester, Westminster – who take four rather than the usual three A levels. But, for the time being, they are the best guide for parents to a school's academic performance.

Most heads would argue that the league tables tell you nothing else. I disagree. The league tables also identify some of the best schools in the country. A selective entry does not automatically translate itself into a high average A level score. Or to put it another way, a bad school cannot produce good examination results, however selective its entry. So a school that is high up the A level league table is by definition a good school, where not only the teaching but the organization, the discipline, the leadership and the staff and pupil morale are also likely to be good.

Yet, it does not follow that the schools lower down the league tables are necessarily bad. The tables can identify some of the best schools; they cannot by their very nature identify all of them. The schools that fill the top fifty places may be among the best in the country, but it is impossible to tell from the league tables where the other outstanding schools are. They may not be in the league table at all; independent schools such as Milton Abbey in Dorset and Shiplake College in Oxfordshire which specialize in helping less academic and less confident pupils to fulfil their potential are unlikely to make the top six hundred if the tables are based on average A level scores.

Neither should you be too impressed by a school's position in the A level pecking order, or by the evidence of one year's results. A school's position may change by forty or more places if its average A level score varies from, say, twenty-one to twenty-two. The average position over five years would be much more revealing. As in a golf tournament, it is the schools that can post a good score year after year who are the real champions.

League tables also help parents make direct comparisons between state and independent schools in their area. This is where the government's version of the results is more useful because schools are listed by local authority. What it shows is that there are certain parts of the country where it would be madness to pay fees for an independent school in the expectation of better A level results.

Other widely-held beliefs are challenged by the league tables.

Boarding numbers are falling and it is assumed that as the schools are forced to become less selective their academic standard will compare less and less favourably with that of the day schools. The tables show that this is true of the weaker boarding schools, but they also show how well some boarding schools are doing academically, even when they do not know until the first day of term whether all their beds will be filled. Seven of the top twenty schools in the 1995 A level table were boarding schools, including the top school, Winchester. That is remarkable and reinforces the view that they must be very good schools indeed. How else can we explain the margin by which girls' boarding schools such as Wycombe Abbey and St Mary's, Calne, outperform so many girls' day schools with highly selective entries?

The league tables also help to raise academic standards by putting pressure on heads and teachers to bring out the best in their pupils. I am sure most schools thought they were doing that anyway, but it is surprising what a difference the prospect of public comparison with your rivals can make. Nor are these improvements made at the expense of a rounded education, as is often alleged. One of the most striking characteristics of the most successful academic schools is that they still manage to offer their pupils such a wide range of interests and so many fields in which to excel. Educating the whole person is not the prerogative of schools with modest academic pretensions, as many of those schools' prospectuses sometimes suggest.

The ill-effects of league tables are to be found not in the narrowing of pupils' horizons but in the tactics some heads employ to improve their school's position. Some independent schools enter weaker pupils as private candidates for A level – so that the poor grades do not bring down the school's average score – but this practice is not widespread. The temptation to concentrate on borderline candidates at GCSE is stronger. When the government's version of the results makes no distinction between an A grade and a C grade, how the abler pupils are getting on may seem comparatively unimportant.

Schools may also be tempted to discourage borderline candidates from taking the harder A level courses; or from staying on for A level at all.

Although league tables are blamed for encouraging these tactics, the truth is that schools with an academic reputation have for a long time been tempted to put the interests of the school before the interests of the individual. The most notorious example was the way in which top independent schools geared their whole academic programme to the needs of pupils who were likely to win scholarships to Oxford and Cambridge, which was the public measure of a school's academic performance at the time, and largely ignored the needs of the other A level candidates.

The mixture of hostility and astute public relations that characterizes the head's response to academic league tables should not blind you to the fact that the tables, despite their limitations, provide you with much useful information. As new tables appear, based on Key Stage tests in state schools and on subject areas, such as science and modern languages at A level, the information available to parents will become even more useful. It will never give you the whole picture, but you know that. What surprises me is that so many headmasters and headmistresses assume that you don't.

Yours sincerely,
John Rae

9 What do we need to know about schools in Scotland before we move there?

Dear David and Katherine

The public examinations and the educational traditions are different in Scotland. There are, however, independent schools that take English exams and follow the English public school tradition, though they are less 'English' now and attract fewer pupils from south of the border. The majority of Scottish independent schools sit Scottish exams and have inherited a different tradition, which is both more democratic and more single-mindedly academic.

When you mention that you are moving to Scotland with your young family, people will probably tell you how lucky you are. The contrast between the conviction that the Scots take education seriously and the English do not, is firmly lodged in the popular mind. You could say that the Scots have always taken education seriously, while the English have only recently realized the importance of doing so. If that is true, the reason is rooted in religion. For, unlike the Church of England, Scottish Calvinism believed that universal education was necessary 'for the preservation of religion'. While the English educated the offspring of the ruling elite, the Scots set up an academy or grammar school in every town which became the focus of local pride and as close as it was possible to come, prior to the social reforms of the twentieth century, to a national education system. The hunger for education in Scotland may not have been as keen as later generations imagined, but the highly-respected schoolmaster or 'dominie' and the children who trudged miles daily through all weathers to attend his school really did exist.

How far this tradition has been modified, I find it hard to judge. Many of the leading independent schools – Dundee High School, Robert Gordon's College in Aberdeen, George Watson's College in Edinburgh and Hutchesons' Grammar School in Glasgow – still adhere strongly to this Scottish tradition. The pre-eminent state schools would argue that they do, too, and that 'going comprehensive' is consistent with the ideal of universal education. The independent schools founded on the English model, such as Fettes College in Edinburgh, stand outside this tradition – they are more likely to have a majority of pupils boarding and taking English exams – but there is no great philosophical divide between independent schools that reflect the various traditions, because all independent schools now have a common concern to help their pupils obtain the best possible academic qualifications.

There are, as you would expect, good and bad schools in both sectors, but in terms of academic achievement the foremost state schools are not treading on the heels of the good independent schools as they are in England. The state schools command widespread loyalty for political, rather than for academic, reasons. In a country where the political map is dominated by the Labour Party, the proportion of children who attend independent schools is less than half of that in England. For the same reason state schools in Scotland do not opt out of local authority control – there are only two grant maintained schools in Scotland – so that particular route to greater independence is effectively closed. For the high-powered, academic independent schools, such as Hutchesons' Grammar School, there is no effective competition from the state sector.

Individual state schools command loyalty on their own merits. In Edinburgh, James Gillespie's High School may not be the school it once was when Miss Jean Brodie was in her prime – it is now co-educational and comprehensive – but it is still the first choice of many middle-class parents for their daughters. Only when girls fail to win a place at James Gillespie's do their parents reluctantly consider opting for an independent school.

Your decision whether to send your children to an independent school will be influenced by other factors. There are no independent schools in the Highland Region and only one in the Borders. Even in major towns, such as Inverness and Oban, the choice is between the local state school or independent boarding school. There are very few Roman Catholic independent schools and comparatively few single-sex independent schools. The proportion of co-educational schools and all-through schools taking children from three to eighteen is higher than in England. Co-education is well established in the Scottish independent sector, so there are fewer mixed sixth forms and more genuine co-educational schools. The first co-educational independent school in Britain was not Bedales as the English suppose, but Dollar Academy, north of Stirling, which was founded as a co-educational school in 1818, long before Bedales first admitted girls in 1898, and exactly a hundred and fifty years before Marlborough believed it was breaking new ground by admitting girls to its sixth form.

Comparing the academic performance of independent schools in Scotland is as difficult as it would be to construct an academic league table, because there are two examination systems being used concurrently. Scottish Highers are not the equivalent of English A levels (though newspapers often refer to them as such). The Scottish examination system is based on the Standard Grade exam which is taken at fifteen, which is similar to the English GCSE, and the Higher Grade exam which is different from English A level in that it is taken in five or six subjects, not three, and can be taken in one year, or alternatively spread over two. At the independent day schools the brighter pupils take their Highers in one year and then stay at school to take a Certificate of Sixth Year Studies in three or more subjects.

The great advantage of Highers over A level is that pupils are not required to drop key subjects in order to specialize. In England, a pupil can concentrate on A level Latin, Greek and Ancient History, but in Scotland the same pupil would study English, Mathematics and a modern language as well. The Scottish system has the added advantage that senior boys and girls have a final year at school with their main public exams out of the way, which explains why senior pupils in Scottish independent schools are more effectively involved in helping the head to run the school than is the case in England.

Nevertheless, some parents are convinced that the English examination system is better, particularly for those pupils who wish to go to an English university. English universities do accept Scottish Highers (just as Scottish universities accept A levels), but their offer of a place will often be dependent upon the candidate also obtaining certain grades in the Certificate of Sixth Year Studies. So that while parents are wrong to believe that A levels give pupils a better chance of a place at an English university, they are right in thinking that the A level route is less complicated.

In Scotland, the academic leaders of the education system are the independent day schools, as they would be in England, if it were not for the handful of prestigious and academically successful boarding schools. The independent boarding schools in Scotland are not in that class, but they have other qualities which may appeal to you. Loretto College in Musselburgh and Merchiston Castle School in Edinburgh, for example, are not behind the times educationally, but they are a little old-fashioned in the manners and discipline they expect of their pupils.

A year or two ago, I was asked to talk to the boarders at Loretto about alcohol. The talk was scheduled for eight o'clock on a Saturday evening, a time when at English boarding schools the juniors would have their feet up watching a video and the seniors would be enjoying alcohol, with or without the head's permission. The boys and girls at Loretto wore uniform, listened attentively and behaved courteously. I can think of very few boarding schools in England where the discipline is good enough for the head to risk requiring the boarders to turn out on a Saturday evening in uniform to listen to a visiting speaker.

Your strategy for your children's education should, as in England, be based on identifying the best available secondary schools. You may find the heads of state secondary schools as reluctant as elsewhere to tell you which are the successful feeder primary schools. The publication of national test results provides useful information, but there is no substitute for local knowledge. Do not make the mistake of choosing a primary school when you are 300 miles away.

You will need to start planning earlier than in England. In Scotland children start their full-time education six months earlier at the age of four and a half and the cut-off date is 1st March, not 1st September. Children stay in primary school for seven years, not six, and enter their secondary school six months later than in England, at about twelve.

If you decide that the best available secondary schools are independent, your choice for the early years will be influenced by the high proportion of all-through schools. Many of the leading independent day schools educate pupils from the age of three to eighteen. You will need to check in each case whether that is a 'seamless' education with no internal examinations which your children have to pass to qualify for the next stage. In contrast to the independent all-through schools in England which are almost all girls' schools, those in Scotland are mostly co-educational. I assume that this explains why so few pupils wish to change schools in the sixth form. All-through schools also recruit direct from state primary schools at twelve, so that route into a good independent day school is open to you.

Independent boarding schools in Scotland are flexible about the age of entry, as they need to be. They face the same decline in boarding school numbers as in England. Some have their own preparatory departments, but most are only too happy to recruit pupils from state primary schools.

Scotland lacks really high-powered, academic boarding schools, but its independent sector is in other respects as strong and diverse as England's. There are schools which excel in providing assistance for pupils with learning difficulties, such as dyslexia, and schools that help less academic pupils to exceed expectations. An interesting addition is the New School in Dunkeld, a weekly boarding school which caters for children who are not only less academic, but also too 'educationally fragile' to flourish in mainstream schools. The tradition of sporting excellence also continues. My first teaching experience was at an independent school in Edinburgh where it was unusual for the rugby fifteen not to include two or three future internationals. Former independent school pupils still play a larger part in international rugby than is the case in England or Wales.

Perhaps the most interesting characteristic of these schools is the almost total absence of the snobbish overtones that still cling to some independent schools in England. Their clientele is predominantly middle class, but in line with Scotland's educational tradition their ethos is meritocratic rather than elitist.

Scotland's independent sector has an impact and prestige out of proportion to its size, especially in the major centres of population. One consequence is that in these centres – Glasgow, Edinburgh and Aberdeen – the state schools find it hard to compete; or to put it another way, the state schools are almost certainly better than their examination results suggest because the independent day schools have 'creamed off' many of the more able pupils. In Aberdeen, for example, the best state school, Aberdeen Grammar School, would surely have better results if it was not competing with the highly successful independent school, Robert Gordon's College. It is no surprise to find that the most successful state school in the Higher Grade examinations is in the Shetland Islands – as far away as possible from the competition of the independent schools.

The best source of information on independent schools is Scotland's branch of the Independent Schools Information Ser-

vice (ISIS) in Edinburgh. For state secondary schools, the best
starting point is the results of Standard and Higher Grade
examinations published in November. *The Scotsman* news-
paper publishes a three-year comparison, region by region, as
well as the results of independent schools over the same period.

Your children will not be at a disadvantage moving to Scotland. There will be some limitations to your choice, such as
fewer state secondary schools and independent boarding
schools that are strongly academic, but your children will have
access to an educational tradition and to a structure of public
examinations that are in some respects superior to those in
England. If you can choose where to live and can afford to
pay fees, Edinburgh has the highest concentration of good
independent schools in the United Kingdom.

Yours sincerely,
John Rae

10 Can the right strategy guarantee the right outcome?

Dear Dr and Mrs Llewellyn

However carefully you plan, you cannot remove the element of chance from your children's education. Elements of chance exist in any environment, but a child's education is particularly vulnerable to what might be called 'the luck of the draw'.

For example, in an academic girls school, Natasha 'hated mathematics' and, although she was doing well in other subjects, seemed likely to fail or do poorly in GCSE maths, thus spoiling what would otherwise be a string of A grades to put on her university application form. By chance, Natasha's maths teacher left at the start of the GCSE year. Mrs Smith, who had never succeeded in enabling Natasha to understand, was replaced by Mrs Owen, who quickly spotted Natasha's problem and within a few weeks had begun to turn Natasha's dislike of the subject into the self-confidence that comes from understanding. Whereas Mrs Smith had been distant and impatient with girls who had difficulties, Mrs Owen was easy to approach and always willing to explain. At the end of the year, Natasha obtained an A grade in maths.

Variations on this theme, sometimes working in the child's favour and sometimes not, could be told by parents all over the world. Yet the element of chance in education has never, as far as I am aware, been the subject of study. Educationalists and head teachers are reluctant to acknowledge its existence. Educationalists like to believe their subject is a science in which chance has no place. Headmasters and headmistresses know only too well how important the element of chance is, but to discuss it openly with parents would be to admit that not all their staff were good enough.

Most people in the school think that Mrs Owen is a better maths teacher than Mrs Smith, but if you are a head it is not an opinion you can afford to endorse, certainly not in public. You are the head of a team. You may encourage teachers to improve their performance, fire warning shots across the lazy and dismiss the incompetent, but you cannot tell parents that their daughter's chance of a good grade in GCSE maths largely depends on whose class she is in. That would be bad for the team's morale. It also leaves you vulnerable to demands from parents that their children should change from one class to another, a request you cannot agree to because Mrs Owen would have an impossibly large class, while Mrs Smith could end up with no class at all.

We all want our children to be taught by good teachers – all the time. In other words, we want the element of chance to be removed. But we know from our own experience of school that there are never enough good teachers. The element of chance can be reduced, but not eliminated. Even the best independent and state schools have some poor teachers. They are not bad enough to dismiss, but they are not good enough to teach your child as well as you would wish. No headmaster can put his hand on his heart and say, 'I have a first-class teaching staff in every department and no weaknesses'.

If this is true of the best schools, there will also be schools at the other end of the spectrum where poor teachers are in the majority. When politicians assure us that the vast majority of teachers in our schools are dedicated professionals, I am sceptical; there *are* many such teachers, but I doubt whether they are 'the vast majority'. Clearly, the better the school, the greater the chance that most of your children's teachers, including the head teacher, will be good at their job.

When headteachers leave, the change of leadership also has

an impact on the pupils. A new broom may sweep away the poor teachers and disruptive pupils, but a new head who hits out blindly to fulfil his promise to the governors to tighten discipline is dangerous. I have seen peccadilloes punished with expulsion to demonstrate a new head's fitness to rule. A new head, who is incompetent as well as capricious, can turn the good school you chose into a bad school you would never have chosen in a remarkably short time.

In a boarding school, the choice of housemaster or house-mistress is also critical to your child's development. Yet, a good housemaster or housemistress who is helping your child navigate the rough water of the teenage years may be appointed to a headship, only to be replaced by someone who does not understand how deeply and powerfully the currents of adolescence can run.

The element of chance may also operate in a perverse way. I have known teachers who have inspired such loyalty to their subject that they have, in effect, hijacked their pupils' careers. A charismatic teacher may persuade a pupil to read the wrong subject at university, in the sense that, when the pupil leaves school, he discovers too late that it was to the teacher, not the subject, that he was committed. What appeared to the parents to be their son's good fortune in having an inspiring teacher turned out to be to the boy's disadvantage.

Your children may also be unlucky in their school contemporaries. A few strong, extrovert personalities may exert an influence for good or ill over a class, even over a whole year. Parents try to have some say in their children's school contemporaries by paying fees or targeting a good state school, but the phenomenon of the 'bad year' can occur in any school.

One of our grandchildren is in what his school describes as a 'bright but difficult group'. In other words, the teachers find it hard to discipline them. Form detentions are the preferred solution. It is up to the school to sort out the troublemakers and restore order. Meanwhile, we all give him advice, 'keep your head down' – that sort of thing. We are acknowledging the role that chance must play.

As it is a good school, the headmaster will ensure that chance does not damage our grandson's education. He may not be as lucky as Natasha's headmistress – for whom Mrs Smith's departure was a stroke of good fortune. Chance lays its hand on headteachers too. I remember the excitement I felt when an uninspiring teacher said it was all too much for him and he thought he would have to resign. It was probably a cry for help, but I told him to put his resignation on paper. You may disapprove, but the pupils benefited.

Our grandson's headmaster will not wait for a stroke of good fortune. Sooner or later he will replace the form teacher, or move in himself to identify and punish the ringleaders. Isn't that what we expect of a good school?

We should not be surprised that chance plays an important role in education. What children learn is the result of a complex pattern of encounters and relationships with many individuals over a long period of time. Most of us have the good fortune to be taught by at least one outstanding teacher, who seems in retrospect to have made all the difference to the development of our interests and enthusiasms. The better the school, the more such teachers there are. And, of course, that is one of the reasons to move heaven and earth to get your children into a good school.

No school mentions chance in the prospectus. 'With any luck your child will get a good education here' is not much of a sales pitch. But knowing that is the real situation helps parents to identify some of the key questions to ask about the school. If there are frequent changes of staff and a high proportion of part-time or unqualified teachers, the chances of your children being taught badly are greater. If the discipline is poor, the chances of the authorities doing something when your children's classes are disrupted are less. The more carefully you choose the school, the more chance that your children will be taught maths by a Mrs Owen rather than a Mrs Smith.

Your strategy cannot eliminate the element of chance in your children's schooling, but it can load the dice in their favour.

But what do you do if, despite your careful choice of school, your child's education is being held back by a bad teacher? Before complaining, make sure of your facts by checking with the parents of other children in the same class. A complaint carries more weight if it is made by a group of parents, and as the member of a group you will be less worried about your child being blamed.

As I have explained, heads are reluctant to acknowledge that one teacher is better than another. They are even more reluctant to acknowledge that a teacher is no good at all. So do not be surprised if the first reaction to your complaint is a defensive one.

The headmaster's position on this type of issue is difficult. Unless he is incompetent, he will be well aware of this teacher's failings and will have tried to do something about them. If neither he nor the head of the academic department has been able to bring about an improvement, the question of finding a replacement will have been discussed. But a teaching staff is not a football team, a poor performer cannot be replaced immediately by another member of the squad. However sympathetic the head is to your complaint, he knows his chances of finding a better teacher at short notice are slim. It may be next term, or the term after that, before a satisfactory replacement can be found.

In the meantime, the head must do all in his power to limit the damage to the pupils' education. While recognizing the practical difficulties he faces, you have a right to know what temporary, alternative arrangements he is making. If the head refuses to take any action or even denies there is a problem, you should take your complaint to the chair of the governing body or to a parent governor.

The best laid plans are subject to chance. Like a general watching his strategy unfold, you do not want to interfere too much, but you must be prepared to intervene decisively if you are sure things are going wrong. In the past, when qualifications mattered less, British parents accepted bad teaching as philosophically as they accepted bad weather. But not any longer. There is too much at stake.

Yours sincerely,
John Rae

Part Two

CONSIDERING A SCHOOL

11 How can parents ever really know what a school is like?

Dear Peter and Caroline

I remember being amazed at how little prospective parents wanted to know. They appeared to assume that because Westminster had a good reputation and was difficult to get into, there was nothing further to discuss. But would I have told them the whole truth if they had asked?

Would it have been wise to tell them that although six housemasters were good at their job, one was not and I had found no way of removing him; or that for boys and girls who wished to study most subjects the teaching was excellent, but that this was not true of every academic department? If parents had asked me about the extent of illegal drug use would I have given them the true picture, or one of those honest dishonesties much favoured by headmasters: 'I have no doubt some pupils use illegal drugs, but they are a small minority and they know better than to bring the drugs into the school'?

There are layers of truth about a school. You may penetrate the glossy outer layer of the school prospectus, and decode the headmaster's carefully crafted answers, but there are aspects of the school's life that will elude all but the most searching enquiries. These are not necessarily to the school's discredit; some of the best things a school does, such as one-to-one teaching after hours, are the least likely to be discovered by prospective parents. Some years ago, I was in Winchester, walking back late to my host's house after dinner in the

College, when I happened to look in at a lighted window and saw a master and pupil, sitting on either side of the fire, engaged in what appeared to be an animated discussion about some point in an essay the boy was holding in his hand.

You will not find that in the prospectus, nor will you find out what it is like to be a new boy or girl in a school. Talking with current parents may help, but they do not know as much as you might expect and they may tell you conflicting stories about the same school. Just as there are different layers of truth about a school, so there are true stories that contradict one another. One pupil's experience of the same school, even of the same teachers, may be quite different from another's. The parents of the first will urge you to send your son or daughter, because they have nothing but praise for the school and its staff, while the parents of the second will try to warn you off with tales of incompetence or worse.

The difficulty of really knowing a school should not deter you from finding out all you can. The starting point for most parents will be the school's reputation. But it should only be a starting point because reputations may be undeserved or out of date. In the United States, the jargon of the market place describes some independent schools as 'hot' and others as 'cold'. Hot schools are on the way up, cold schools on the way down. In Britain, the reputation of individual independent schools is more volatile than it has ever been. The hot schools include many unfamiliar names which were not even regarded as 'public schools' a generation ago, while for schools that once held their heads high the market has gone cold. Famous names may still seem attractive if you are in a position to choose them, but a famous name is not a guarantee of high standards. Of the nine schools identified by the Clarendon Commission as the leading public schools in the mid-nineteenth century, only Eton, Winchester, Westminster and St Paul's are still in the leading group and that is because they are good schools, not because they are well known. With all schools it is the current reputation not the historical record that should interest you. Some independent schools invent histories to impress parents. But I'm sure you already know that. It's all pretty harmless, though if they invent their origins one wonders what else they are prepared to invent.

To find out you need a copy of the school prospectus. As a general rule, the more a school is in demand the less money it feels the need to spend on its prospectus. An expensive production should at least alert you to the possibility that the school is short of pupils.

The important thing to remember about any prospectus is that it is a sales document and not an objective assessment of what the school has to offer. Some independent schools produce a video prospectus which is even more subjective. Whether it is an independent school or a state school – for the latter, too, are now obliged to sell their education to prospective parents and pupils – you should no more expect a prospectus to tell you the whole truth than you would expect a holiday brochure to tell you that the hotel in Spain is adjacent to a motorway.

Keeping that in mind, you will have little difficulty reading between the lines and spotting when the school is making a virtue of necessity. A Christian foundation which welcomes boys and girls 'from a wide variety of cultures and backgrounds' has almost certainly been forced to fill empty beds by recruiting in the Middle East and Far East. 'A healthy and secure environment' probably means that the school is some way off the beaten track.

Schools are also prone to use the prospectus to undermine the competition by playing on parental fears. I rather like this dig at city schools from an independent boarding school in stockbroker Surrey: 'It has easy access to London, so that galleries, theatres and concert halls may be visited and enjoyed without prompting parental misgivings about growing up in a London school and a generally urban environment'. Big schools hint at the limitations of small schools and vice versa, while others manage to suggest they have the best of both worlds: 'It is a school large enough to provide huge scope and choice in its many academic and extra-curricular activities and yet small enough to be a family, where every child has a sense of belonging and loyalty, of individuality and security'.

'Do not expect heads to be super-salesmen', the Independent Schools Information Service warns parents. 'They have been trained to teach rather than to sell their school.' Maybe, but they learn the art of salesmanship pretty quickly.

I do not know what you will make of the prospectuses you happen to see. As public relations vehicles they can disguise as much as they reveal. Beware of prospectuses which contain beautiful colour photographs and enthusiastic quotes from pupils past and present but few facts. I think you should be wary, too, of the declaration of aims and mission statements. In so far as these describe the school's distinctive ethos they are helpful, but some of them are overflowing with platitudes and too obviously designed to appeal to *every* possible view of what education is about. It is refreshing, therefore, to find a more down-to-earth approach in the prospectus of Yateley School, a state comprehensive in Hampshire: 'The emphasis is very much on academic achievement. Children come to Yateley to learn and teachers to teach'.

It is a *good* school you are looking for, not a high-sounding philosophy of education. I would rather send my child to a good school whose philosophy I disliked than to a mediocre school of whose philosophy I approved. So I would be happy to be spared the school's mission statement if I could have the following factual information: a breakdown of the A level and GCSE results for the last five years, department by department, so that I could identify where the school's academic strengths and weaknesses lay; a copy of the school rules, together with the normal sanctions and punishments; a copy of the school's written policy on bullying and on illegal drugs, the latest inspector's report and a copy of the school's development plan.

You may think this is asking a bit much, but each of these items is provided by some schools so there is no reason why they should not be provided by all. Copies of the inspector's report can be obtained from the Office for Standards in Education (OFSTED), but I would be more impressed if a school provided them automatically to prospective parents.

Whether you will find it easy to extract this additional information may depend on whether the school needs your custom or not. Despite greater openness, the old reluctance to tell parents too much about the school remains. And when there is fierce competition for places, parents may be equally reluctant to ask for fear of jeopardizing their child's chances. The latter should depend on ability alone, but in every entrance exam there are borderline cases and a child whose parents are regarded as potentially 'difficult' is bound to be at a disadvantage.

In a seller's market, the arrogance of the popular schools – both state and independent – may be hard for you to accept, but I would not challenge it head-on if I were you. Try to find out what you need to know in other ways. Current parents are a useful source, as long as you consult enough of them. As I have explained, one enthusiastic or disenchanted parent cannot give you a balanced opinion. St Bees School in Cumbria publishes the names, addresses and telephone numbers of twelve sets of parents who are prepared to be quizzed about the school, a common practice in the United States, but it is still unusual in this country.

For independent schools which recruit at thirteen, the heads of preparatory schools are probably the best source of information. They may not *always* be objective about senior schools with whom they need to maintain good relations, but they do receive regular feedback from former pupils and parents and can give a shrewder judgement than anyone else looking in from the outside. The heads of state primary schools are less well informed about schools which recruit at eleven.

A school's attitude to visits by prospective parents is also influenced by the demand for places. For some urban day schools, the number of applicants makes it impossible to see parents on an individual basis. These schools hold open days for you and your child to see the school, meet some of the pupils and hear from the head and other members of the senior management team. It is an introduction to the school, not an insight into what the school is really like.

Some independent day schools and almost all independent boarding schools like to see parents individually. If this occurs, do not assume that they are looking for customers; schools that have plenty of applicants may still prefer to have personal contact with prospective pupils and their parents. The best school in the world may be the wrong school for a particular child and it is much better to spot the mismatch in advance. The top boarding schools are also drawing on a limited pool of talented children whose parents can afford boarding fees, so the personal touch is part of the recruiting strategy.

The personal touch is even more important to those boarding schools that are short of pupils. Here you will have a chance to spend time asking the head about the school and making your own assessment of his or her qualities, something that parents with children in over-subscribed day schools may never have a chance to do.

I shall write to you separately about getting the most out of a visit to a school. The visit will be an important part of your intelligence gathering, but do not pin on it all your hopes of discovering what the school is really like. No school worth considering will yield all its secrets at the first encounter. Nor is a visit to one school much use in isolation. Even if you have set your heart on that school, make sure that you visit at least two or three more; it is the contrasts that are most revealing.

You can never know a school inside out, but you can and should assemble enough evidence to decide between one school and another. It is essential to set about the task in a methodical way and to work as a team. For husbands to leave the donkey work to their wives and then insist on having the final say is almost certainly a formula for choosing the wrong school. By sharing the task of finding out all that you can about each school you will greatly increase the chances of making a good choice.

How far you should share the task with your children is an interesting question. At eleven or thirteen (but not five or seven), boys and girls can and do have opinions about the schools you are considering. They gather information from visits and open days, pick up rumours in the primary or preparatory school and discuss the relative merits of schools with their friends. Friends and friendliness are probably uppermost in their minds as they prepare to leave their small and familiar world. When children are asked why they would prefer to go to a particular senior school, the answer most frequently given is that it is friendly. And, of course, they naturally want to go where their friends are going.

There is no reason to believe that a school's reputation for being friendly is false; the children's grapevine is at least as reliable as the parents'. But how important is friendliness compared with, say, academic excellence, and how much weight should you give to your child's preference?

A 1995 survey of 1000 girls in their first year at independent day schools run by the Girls Public Day School Trust found that of those who had entered the school at eleven, 59 per cent had made the final choice of school themselves. In 32 per cent of cases the parents made the final choice after consulting their daughter. In very few cases did the daughter play little or no part in the decision.

I think the parents who consulted their daughter but made the final choice themselves were right. However intelligent and perceptive your children are, they cannot take the long view, nor will they find it easy to understand that what is best for their friends may not be best for them. But, if you are going to make the final choice yourself, you should make that clear early on. Don't give your daughter the impression that she is making the choice, only to overrule her when she makes the 'wrong' one.

Whoever makes the choice the ultimate responsibility for

the decision is yours. If the school turns out not to be so friendly after all, you cannot shrug your shoulders and say to your daughter, 'Well, you chose it'.

Not that you would. But the question of how friendly a school is illustrates both the limitations of the child's view and the difficulty that both parents and children have in discovering what a school is really like. Schools go out of their way to be welcoming on open days, but school life does not consist of open days. In the everyday routine of hard work, as well as in the rough-and-tumble of the pupils' underworld, relations will not always be friendly. That is true of good schools as well as bad.

All I am saying is that parents should be looking constantly behind the outward impression that schools project, a skill which children are less well placed to do. The friendliness the child sees may reflect the efficiency with which the school is run and the trouble it takes to make visitors feel welcome. On the other hand, it may reflect a casual, even slack, regime. *You* will recognize the difference between the two, but I wonder whether your daughter will.

Yours sincerely
John Rae

12 How can we make the most of our chance to visit the school?

Dear Peter and Caroline

First, keep your eyes and ears open. A school is alive with clues, but you won't pick them up if you just stroll through the building exchanging pleasantries with your guide. You are not making a social call; you are making a diagnosis, looking for symptoms of the school's good health or sickness.

Secondly, think carefully about how you interpret the evidence. It may sound obvious, but the clues that you pick up and the documents you are given are of little use unless you can place the correct interpretation on them. Like the doctor who gives you your annual check-up, you will have statistical data as well as your own observations, the patient's blood pressure and his nervous twitch, A level results and the graffiti on the headmaster's notice board. What do they tell you?

Your chances of picking up useful clues are much greater if you visit the school as individuals on a normal working day, as opposed to being one of the crowd on an open day. The best time is usually during the morning when classes are being taught, not during an afternoon when in many independent schools the pupils are scattered over the playing fields and the classrooms are empty. If your visit overlaps the mid-morning break so much the better; when the pupils run wild and the teachers seek the safety of the staff room, you will learn more about the values of the school than from the mission statement in the prospectus.

So much for the preliminaries. You arrive at the appointed time. If your appointment is with the headmaster, take his measure. What you are looking for is 'authority'. Of all the qualities we may wish to find in our children's headmaster or headmistress – understanding of the young, integrity, energy, vision – the ability to command respect and obedience is the most important. Without it a community of hundreds of adolescents will fall apart and no amount of ideals and good intentions will hold it together.

Heads come in all shapes and sizes. They are good men and women on the whole, doing their best, though varying in quality to an extent that is not always obvious on the surface. A small, quietly-spoken woman may have a will of iron and the ability to inspire pupils and staff, whereas a striking figure of a man with a gleam in his eye and the latest educational research at his fingertips may well be a fraud.

Many prospective parents are predisposed to trust heads, or at least to be a little in awe of them. Even as adults we are not at ease in the headmaster's study. Yet so much depends on the head's leadership that you must try to assess what sort of man or woman you are dealing with. In some schools, particularly the oversubscribed urban day schools, it may not be clear who is interviewing whom, but whatever the scenario you should not be afraid of asking difficult or searching questions.

In the less-fashionable day schools and boarding schools you will need to be in a sceptical frame of mind when you meet the head. Beware of charm. It is second nature to some headmasters. They are political animals. What headmistresses may lack in plausibility they make up for in directness. I have a suspicion that a headmistress is more likely to tell you the truth, take it or leave it, whereas a headmaster is more likely to have reduced honesty to a fine art, or in some cases to a blunt instrument. 'Come in, ask anything, see anything,' I heard a headmaster tell parents, 'and don't believe everything I say.' He would not have been out of place on the pavements of Soho.

A more subtle use of honesty is the disarming confession. By admitting that something comparatively unimportant needs improving – 'Frankly, our craft, design and technology department is not as dynamic as I would like' – the head hopes to persuade you that what he tells you on more sensitive issues – 'Bullying occurs in every school, but we have a policy for dealing with it quickly and effectively' – is true.

But let us leave him in his study and take a look at the school. Don't be too impressed by the pupils who show you round. They are good company, but they are hand picked. Schools are shrewd to provide pupil guides; there is a limit to what in all fairness you can ask them. Whoever shows you round you should insist on seeing a class in action, preferably fourteen to fifteen year olds, not well-scrubbed new boys. Count the number of desks or pupils to check the school's claims about class size. I see no reason to be shocked or pleased if there are rows of individual desks rather than tables arranged in a less traditional pattern. Bad schools make a fetish of such things. How the classroom is arranged is of little importance compared with the quality of teaching and discipline.

Assessing the standards of teaching on a visit is difficult; a searching question to the head will probably result in a blandly reassuring answer. Clues about discipline are easier to spot. Fourteen to fifteen years olds do not go out of their way to make a favourable impression on visitors, but you will be able to tell the difference between normal adolescent bolshiness and the sour mood that pervades a badly disciplined school.

Poor discipline turns schools sour because pupils and teachers do not know where they stand. If you cannot always see it in their faces, in the way they move around the school and in the way they react to your being there, you will see it in the state of the buildings. Schools cannot be expected to be spick and span like naval ships, but neither should they look like run-down seaside resorts out of season.

Dirty windows and broken furniture, old notices flapping in the wind, graffiti which no one has bothered to remove, all suggest that the authorities lack both the will and the pride to run the school efficiently. Don't be fobbed off with excuses about lack of resources. You need resources to repair a roof, but not to remove graffiti.

Too many locked doors is a bad sign. Some doors, in the science block for example, have to be locked, but a head who needs a large bunch of keys to show you round is running a prison not a school.

Schools have a difficult balance to strike between freedom and order. There is more than one valid way of striking the balance and you may find having visited several different schools that one style appeals to you more than another. Boys' shirt tails hanging out and girls' hair all over the place do not automatically mean the discipline is poor, but if they offend you it is probably wise to look elsewhere. Unless, of course, it is in every other way the best school for your child, in which case you should ignore appearances. Pupils in urban day schools will always look scruffier than their contemporaries in rural boarding schools; they have to run the gauntlet of the city's streets. But there are extremes of appearance and behaviour which should put any parent off. If the pupils are so yobbish that even the teachers appear afraid of them, or so buttoned-up you suspect they dare not step out of line or think for themselves, something is fundamentally wrong.

I wish I could be more precise, but we are talking about the feel of a school, the impression that any reasonably acute visitor has that the school is running either well or badly.

Although the feel is more important than the facilities, the latter tell you something about the school's priorities as well as its ability to raise capital. Here the leading independent schools have an obvious advantage. They are rich. They do not all have endowments, but they can appeal to a well-heeled constituency of parents and former pupils. Trusts and foundations, too, will give grants to independent schools but are reluctant to give money to schools funded by the state.

Independent schools are rich in other ways. Some have a heritage of fine buildings and prestigious sites. One of the least commented-on differences between independent and state schools is that the former are often in very attractive surroundings. However inconvenient and expensive to maintain, historic buildings at least give a school a sense of identity, though critics might call it a sense of their own importance. Antiquity is not to everybody's taste. One thirteen year old asked by his parents to choose between Westminster and St Paul's chose the latter because he found Westminster 'more like a museum than a school'. Buildings and surrounding do matter to some children, but I doubt whether it is wise to make them a decisive factor in your choice. An attractive setting is a bonus; it does not in itself create a good school. Some outstandingly good schools, both state and independent, operate in Dickensian buildings and on restricted sites.

You do not need my guidance on what facilities you should expect to find, but some facilities are more revealing than others. The library, for example, should be the heart of the school during the working day and in a boarding school its lights should be burning well into the evening. Ask how many books there are. A good independent boarding school library will have around 25–30,000 books and a good day-school library about half that number. State school libraries are comparable in size to those of independent day schools though there are exceptional libraries such as Yateley Comprehensive School in Hampshire which has 35,000 books, as many as Eton. By now, schools should have put the books onto a computer catalogue, the automated library system providing pupils and teachers with quick and easy access.

It is unusual for an independent school not to have a full-time librarian. Ask the librarian how many books are lost each year. Every library loses some, but thefts on a big scale – and thefts they usually are – tell you something about the pupils' attitudes, as does the habit of tearing out the pages they need for their homework.

Though security is necessary nowadays, the library should be a welcoming place where pupils are free to browse. But it should not be an alternative common room with briefcases on the tables and pupils whispering in corners. If the library has a down-beat air, walk over to one of the shelves to see what is available. Obsolete, broken-backed books are like graffiti – you wonder what sort of school it is that cannot be bothered to remove them.

As well as teaching pupils to love books and enjoy reading, the library is the place where they learn how to access information. A well-educated young adult does not know all the answers, but will know where and how to find them. Some schools now call their library the Information Centre. I don't like it, but it helps to underline that the library and the information technology are linked both literally through the school's network and in the minds of the pupils. The latter will expect to find at least one encyclopaedia as well as newspapers and periodicals available on CD-ROM.

Schools are at different stages of developing their information technology. I think what you should be looking for is not a room full of computers which you should take for granted, but evidence that there is a whole school policy for providing information technology. Evidence would include the fact that the school had appointed a head or co-ordinator of information technology, that the school was networked, that there was a rolling programme for bringing all the teaching staff up to date, and, above all, that information technology was being used across the curriculum. 'Computers are in routine use wherever appropriate,' as one prospectus puts it. The place of the Internet in schools and the use of information technology in public exams are both issues that have not been resolved, but you should expect to find each academic department using the available technology in the way that best suits their needs. Early enthusiasts made exaggerated claims about the value of computers in education, just as opponents still express exaggerated fears. However, you can probably be assured that the school has the right approach if you find that information technology is integrated into the work of the school and not marginalized. Are the pupils in the history room using a CD-ROM to study Renaissance art and architecture, or is the computer just an alien presence on the shelf collecting dust?

If you are visiting a boarding school it is particularly important to look behind the facade. What facilities are available to boarders at the weekend is more telling than the brightly-coloured duvets on the dormitory beds. Like the library, the brand-new sports centre is not much use to boarders if it is closed on Sundays. As you go round the boarding houses, look at the notice boards and the walls of the senior pupils' studies. I would not send a child to a school which allowed full-frontal nudes on the study wall. That is not prudishness. If the adults in a school do not know where to draw the line, or are afraid to say so, what is the point of placing a child in their care?

By being alert and interpreting what you see and hear, you begin to get a sense of the reality behind the prospectus and the promotional video. But do not visit the school in a negative frame of mind. You are looking for the good things as well as the bad. The skill is in deciding which ones matter, either to the quality of education as a whole or to your child's needs in particular.

Talk the visit over when you get home while it is fresh in your minds. It is surprisingly easy to put off that discussion, especially if the evidence collected runs counter to your preconceptions. Refusal to believe intelligence that does not endorse your plans, a characteristic of the military mind in the First World War, may lead you to press ahead with a flawed strategy.

On the other hand the visit is only one source of evidence. If a school is at the top of the academic league table, the fact that the classrooms could have done with a coat of paint and the pupils rushed along the corridor rather than standing back to let you pass, is hardly sufficient to make you change your mind.

Yours sincerely
John Rae

13 How much does the head matter?

Dear Tim and Jenny

It was good to hear from you again. I think the head makes all the difference. That may not be true of some other countries where the head is little more than a bureaucrat but, in the British tradition, the head is expected to be both the captain of the ship and the director of the film. On his or her authority and vision everything depends.

The degree to which the head is in command varies from school to school and from head to head. Under the Education Acts of the 1980s, the heads of state schools have less freedom of action than the heads of independent schools, but much hinges on the individual's personality and style. Whatever the law says, a strong-minded head of a state school may, in practice, be more independent of the governing body than the head of an independent school who lacks the self-confidence and political know-how to exploit the greater freedom he or she enjoys.

In an independent school, the governors appoint and dismiss the head. They endorse or modify the head's strategy for the school's development and they oversee the management of the school's finances, but they leave the running of the school to the man or woman they have appointed.

It is not always as clear-cut and tidy as that. But, for the most part, the distinction between the chief executive and the board is maintained. The governors would no more expect to participate in the appointment of staff than would the non-executive directors of a public company.

In a state school, the governors have a right to participate in the appointment of staff – a right which they do not always exercise – and to be involved in matters of discipline and the curriculum. As a number of the governors are required by law to be current parents, the head is bound to feel that there is someone with a vested interest always looking over their shoulder. Just as well, you may say, given the autocratic style of heads in the past.

The head does not need to be autocratic anymore, but he does have to be convincing to an unusual community made up of young people and adults. I doubt whether it is easy for him to achieve this if too many of the important decisions are made by someone else, yet the trend in recent years has been to limit the head's authority.

Educational reforms that have given state schools more control over the management of their affairs and, in the case of grant-maintained schools, independence from the local education authority, have not necessarily strengthened the head's position. On the contrary, because governors are now seen to be publicly accountable for the school's performance and reputation, they may be more inclined to interfere in what should be the head's domain.

The heads of independent schools have not escaped the impact of public accountability and the intensifying competition between schools. The publication of academic league tables and the shortage of boarders have made some governing bodies less detached in their attitude and more prepared to sack the head and appoint a new one if the school's numbers and reputation are declining. Whereas short-term contracts were anathema to heads of independent schools, they are now part of the deal. For the heads of independent and state schools alike these are difficult times.

What is it that the head does that makes all the difference? I have been a pupil, a teacher, a parent and a governor. None of these people can know, as the head must know, all the pieces of the jigsaw. However interested you are as a governor, you are on the outside looking in. However dedicated you are as a teacher, you are on the inside with little time to consider the outside pressures on the school. The head, like the film director, is the only person with the whole thing in his mind.

All successful heads formulate a clear idea of how they would like their school to develop. The vision may be their own, or the result of exhaustive consultation. But whichever it is, only the head can articulate it and give the school the necessary purpose and direction to improve.

The school development plan will not work unless the head believes in it and drives it forward. In a country boarding school in the north of England, a shortage of applicants convinced governors and senior staff that co-education and the admission of day pupils was the best strategy for survival. But the school's new head took a different view. He saw that a great number of rival schools were following the very same strategy and that it was therefore unlikely to provide the upsurge of applicants the school needed. He believed there was still a market for a good single-sex, full-boarding school and he persuaded the governors and senior staff to share his conviction. He was proved right. The school is flourishing because there is now no obvious competitor within a hundred miles.

No other individual or group can provide that sort of leadership to a school. Nor can anyone else set the school's priorities and so profoundly influence its atmosphere. How Peter experiences whichever school he goes to will largely depend on the priorities the head has set and the atmosphere he has created. There are happy schools and unhappy schools and, as in any other organization, the difference is in the quality of the leadership. It is little use the head having vision if he lacks authority. Staff and pupils will make a mockery of his dreams if he cannot inspire their respect. And he will command neither respect nor loyalty if his priorities are wrong. However good he may be at marketing the school or raising funds, it will all be wasted if he loses sight of the fact that the school's primary purpose is not projecting an image but teaching and learning.

For good or ill then, the head does make all the difference, a factor which worries some critics. They argue that the tradition of solo leadership in schools is out of date and that decisions should be arrived at via a democratic process in which all the teachers participate. But who in this participating democracy will ultimately take the hard decisions, and who will stand up at morning assembly and explain to the school why the decisions had to be taken? Perhaps more than any other organization, this community of adolescents and adults needs a leader it can identify and focus upon.

A good head will consult senior colleagues on the staff and carry the governing body with him even if that entails some compromise. But the initiative is his. The governors modify his plans, not vice versa. The senior staff may modify his plans too; he cannot push through an unpopular change if all hands are against him. But he sets the agenda and day by day makes all the important decisions as well as many trivial ones that could be made by others. You would be surprised how reluctant senior and experienced teachers are to make decisions. They prefer the head to give a ruling. And, in turn, heads are reluctant to delegate authority because they know they will be held responsible for everything that happens.

That, in turn, reflects the difficulty of dismissing teachers. The heads of commercial companies delegate authority because they know that they can swiftly replace subordinates who fail. The head of a school can neither measure failure so accurately, nor replace staff so easily.

The result is that more matters are referred to the leader of a school than is the case in other organizations. In a typical week, the head may have to select a new member of staff, decide whether a pupil caught with illegal drugs should be expelled, tell a teacher who cannot control an unruly form that he must get on top of the problem if he wishes to remain, and judge which of two academic departments has the better claim to an additional period that has become available on the timetable. These are the sort of decisions you would expect a head to make. But he may also have to give any number of off-the-cuff rulings – usually of the 'can pupils be excused this, to do that' variety – some of which will come back to haunt him. 'He has stubbornly refused to wear the regulation shoes', a boarding school housemaster once wrote to me, asking for a ruling on whether the boy should be 'allowed to get away with it'.

You might think that heads should have better things to do, but it is in the nature of school life in this country that the head is responsible for seeing more clearly than others which direction the school should take, while dealing on a day-to-day basis with the problems of 'regulation shoes'.

Given that the head exercises such power and influence, particularly in an independent school, prospective parents want to be reassured that the man or woman at the top possesses the right qualities. But would we agree on what those qualities are? Some governing bodies now say they need a head who can market the school, but when pupils are asked, the quality most frequently mentioned is approachability. What makes a successful head is not his marketing skills, or his ease of manner, but his ability to persuade the school to believe in him. In that sense, the ultimate source of his authority is charismatic. He has got what it takes to inspire others.

You won't find that on his curriculum vitae. You might recognize it when you meet him, although don't forget you have to look through the eyes of the pupils and the teachers. Local and parental gossip about the head is based on hearsay. It also tends to be overoptimistic, particularly when a new head arrives. New heads are almost always said to be 'very good', so if you hear that you should take it with a pinch of salt. What they say about the head after four or five years is more revealing.

In the independent sector, the fact that the head is a member of a top schools' organization such as the Headmasters' and

Headmistresses' Conference is reassuring, but it is not a guarantee that he or she has the right qualities. The Conference is a club. Election to membership is based on the school's academic standing, not on the head's ability to do the job. But the Conference, in common with all headteachers' organizations, has accepted the need to provide training courses which at least give new heads some knowledge of the demands that will be made on them. Whether it is possible to produce good heads by encouraging or requiring them to take a professional qualification is a matter of debate. You can imagine how the argument goes back and forth between skills that can be learnt and innate qualities of character, between the competent manager and the charismatic leader, between the right qualifications and the right stuff.

From the parents' point of view this polarization seems unnecessary. Why can't heads be both efficient and charismatic? The most effective heads probably are, though it is unlikely that they would attribute their success to any formal training.

Professional qualifications for headteachers are more highly regarded in state schools than independent schools because the former are more inclined to see the head's role in terms of management than leadership. You should adjust your expectations accordingly. In time, a national professional qualification for headteachers might come to be regarded as a minimum guarantee for parents that the head knows what he has to do. But it would no more guarantee that he is good at his job than a teaching qualification guarantees excellence in the classroom.

While the calibre of the head is of critical importance to parents, they have to take it on trust that the school has selected the best available man or woman for the job. It is a recurring complaint that heads are not what they used to be, but with 23,000 state schools and 2500 independent schools, there never have been enough good heads to go round. Which is why the way heads are selected is so important.

In state schools and independent schools this is the responsibility of the governing body; a responsibility governors have guarded jealously against any suggestion that they might need professional help. It is only in recent years that a few leading independent schools, including Eton, Charterhouse and St Paul's Girls School, have engaged executive recruitment companies to be part of the selection process. The vast majority of governing bodies believe they are well qualified to do the job themselves, with the result that while they may appoint the best candidate who *applies*, they seldom appoint the best person who is *available*.

Governors do not always have a clear idea of how the school should develop and so are unable to match the candidate to the task. They may also be pushing their own candidate, or have a bee in their bonnet about what qualities a head should have, regardless of the school's needs at that time. Their chances of making the right decision are further decreased by the practice of allowing all the governors to have a say in the final selection. 'Plenary selection' means the head may be chosen as a result of the votes of governors who seldom attend meetings and know little about the real needs of the school.

This amateur approach, characteristic of independent schools, does not preclude the possibility of making a good appointment, but it has resulted in some well-known disasters. Executive recruitment companies cannot guarantee a perfect match but, by being much more thorough in drawing up the short list, they increase not only the chances of the best available people applying but also of a successful outcome. Or to put it another way, executive recruiting turns the process of identifying and selecting candidates who match the school's requirements from an amateur into a professional operation.

If I were you, I would be biased in favour of a school that had used an executive recruitment company. At the moment they are few and far between, but by the time Peter goes to secondary school the number will have increased and will include grant maintained schools that have opted out of local authority control. A professional approach is vital in the independent sector where the number of good candidates for headships is falling and the number of heads leaving early is rising. The headships of smaller boarding schools, once seen as stepping-stones for ambitious young men and women, are now regarded as cul-de-sacs. Unless the governors of these schools set about finding a head in a professional manner, those particular schools' decline is likely to accelerate.

There *are* good heads and because they matter so much to the life of the school it is certainly worth trying to identify them. I cannot tell you who the good heads are. You have to make your own assessment based on all the evidence you can gather. Above all, you must meet the headmaster or head-mistress face to face.

Yours sincerely
John Rae

14 Can you send us a list of the obvious and less obvious questions we should ask the head of a secondary school?

Dear Dr and Mrs Buchan

I do not know what sort of secondary schools you have in mind. Most of the questions I have listed are relevant to all secondary schools and you will recognize those that are intended for a particular type. Some of the questions may already have been answered by the schools' prospectuses, but since they might tend to be long on philosophy and short on facts, I have included them.

You are trying to size up the head as well as the school. It is his or her views you want not the latest research findings. If the head begins an answer 'All the latest research shows . . .', you should counter with 'But what is your own opinion?' Here are the obvious questions in no particular order:

1 *May we see a copy of the school rules?*

Having seen the rules, you can then ask supplementary questions about the various punishments the school uses, the rule that is most frequently broken and the rule that the senior pupils seem to resent most. This is a good way of assessing the head's attitude to discipline. He or she knows that discipline is never quite as good as the school – or you – would like. Providing a firm framework, without treating every peccadillo as a test case, is one of a head's most difficult tasks. Mixing your metaphors, you might try asking, 'How do you know when to put your foot down and when to turn a blind eye?' A good headmaster will respond with a wry smile; it is what he asks himself every day.

2 *May we see the GCSE and A level results, by subject, for the last three years?*

You will need time to study the results, but you can tell at a glance if some academic departments are more successful than others. The head's explanation may be that some departments attract the brighter pupils, but that is a circular argument; they attract the brighter pupils because they are good departments. The pupils know exactly who and where the good teachers are. Why not ask the head to name the strongest and weakest academic departments? Weakness in an academic school is relative, but it would still be interesting to know what the head is planning to do about it. The A level results also highlight which departments are hanging on by the skin of their teeth. If only two pupils are studying Russian A level, what arguments does the head use for continuing to make it available?

3 *How does the school's curriculum compare with the National Curriculum?*

Independent schools are not required to follow the National Curriculum. In practice, they aim to offer more not less. To find out what more means, focus on the GCSE years. Does the school offer three separate sciences at GCSE level? What choices are available to GCSE pupils outside the core of compulsory subjects?

In the sixth form, the mark of a good school is not the number of A level *subjects* on offer, but the number of A level *combinations*. Some sixth forms pride themselves on the wide range of subjects that can be studied, but that is of little value to the pupils if some combinations of mainstream subjects are not available. Ask the head, for example, whether it is possible to study history with two modern languages. You cannot know at this stage what subjects your children will want to study in the sixth form, but you can gauge whether the head understands the importance of having the right combinations available.

4 *What do you expect of parents?*

All schools are more open to parents now and the head will be keen to tell you about the many occasions when you and your views will be welcome. You want to look behind this fashionable rhetoric about partnership. The question is designed to enable you to do so. What are the limits of partnership? Is the head bound to welcome you in the school at any time? Are parents and the head on the same side if a pupil is being investigated for the use of illegal drugs? Is it any of the head's business if parents allow at home behaviour they would criticize the school for condoning?

5 *How many teachers are leaving at the end of the year and why?*

Staff turnover, and the reasons for it, is a way of introducing a more fundamental issue. What you are trying to discover is how good the teachers are. You can put the question any number of ways. Every school has some unsatisfactory teachers – how do you deal with this problem? Are all your staff qualified to teach their subject? What is the age profile of your staff? You could even quote A. S. Neill, the ultra-progressive head of Summerhill, who said he was glad none of his former pupils had gone into teaching, it showed how well-adjusted they were. How well-adjusted are your teaching staff, headmaster? Perhaps not, but you do need to obtain some insight into their quality and morale. Does the head find the task of improving his staff a burden or a challenge? If it is a burden you can be pretty sure that the quality and morale are low.

6 *What extras are there to pay on top of fees?*

This is a straightforward question to which there should be a straightforward answer. The reason for asking it is that practice in independent schools varies widely. Some say they 'keep extras to an absolute minimum'; others spell out the extras which can amount to 5 per cent of the boarding fee, and others again say nothing other than that 'full details may be obtained from the Bursar'. Extra tuition in music and academic subjects, books bought by the pupils, medical insurance and coaching for some of the more recherché sports are normally accepted as being outside the fees. But some schools charge extra for laundry, stationery and coaching in mainstream sports such as fencing and sailing. Almost all schools are misleading about voluntary or optional extras. You are bound to pay for a class trip to the theatre, or an expedition to the hills, because you do not want your child to be left out. It is misleading to call these charges optional. When you talk to the head, ask how often these 'optional extras' occur, at what age and at what cost. They are the ones you did not budget for.

7 *Where do your leavers go?*

Most heads will have an analysis of leavers' destinations. It should list all universities, not just Oxford, Cambridge and 'other universities'. Ask how many pupils leave at GCSE and why. An academically selective school should not normally lose pupils at this stage. Are the weaker ones being pushed out to improve the school's position in the A level league table? Are the stronger ones leaving to go to better sixth forms? Are the restless hoping to find a more permissive regime in a sixth form college? Or is it just a case of parents no longer being able to pay the fees? One or two GCSE leavers from a school with a selective entry would not suggest anything wrong; eight or ten every year would.

8 *What are the strengths and weaknesses of your non-academic programme?*

One of the problems in choosing an independent school is that every one of them apparently has a thriving and varied programme of sport and other extra-curricular activities. Can they really be as impressive as they look in the prospectus? Some schools do offer an extraordinary range of such activities for every age group and not just for experts. When a young boy says, 'I hate being bored and enjoy variety, so I take part in a different activity every day of the week', I believe him because I know the school. But you need to check. Although the all-round education is one of the strengths of the independent sector, it is not always as good as it sounds, nor do independent schools have a monopoly of this form of excellence. Many of the best state schools have a good range of successful sporting teams (despite public disquiet about the decline of sport in schools), combined cadet forces and all the music, drama and other activities you would expect to find in a good independent school.

9 *May we see the school's written policy on bullying and the use of illegal drugs?*

Most schools will now have a written policy on both of these important subjects. The head should be willing to show them to you, but do not be surprised if he is reluctant to let you take them away. The reason for asking the head this question is also to discover how this policy works in practice. Both subjects are high on every parent's list, but they are the two subjects on which heads are most likely to be defensive. If the head is cautious in answering your questions, I think you should respect that. Bold assertions about the extent of illegal drug taking or bullying should arouse your suspicion. The head cannot possibly know how many of his pupils use illegal drugs, either occasionally or regularly. He should have a clearer picture of the extent of bullying, but even here much goes unnoticed by authority. An honest head is cautious not because he has something to hide, but because he cannot give the absolute assurance that some parents are seeking.

10 *May we see a copy of the school development plan?*

I am not sure whether this is an obvious or a less obvious question. I would expect most state and independent schools to have a development plan, which would be updated each year. It is not primarily about buildings, but about the plans the head and governors have formulated to ensure the school remains viable and competitive. So it may, for example, include plans to raise academic standards, increase or decrease numbers, go co-educational, admit day pupils to a boarding establishment, or even to merge with a neighbour-ing school, all plans that you as a prospective parent would like to know. There may be circumstances in which the plans are required to be confidential – in the middle of negotiations for a merger, for example – but some heads are unnecessarily secretive. They are not manufacturers protecting a new prod-uct from the prying eyes of their competitors and should be prepared to talk you through the development plan, even if the document remains out of sight. The heads of independent schools are more reluctant than the heads of state schools to show you a copy of the school's development plan, no doubt because in some cases the plan does not exist.

11 *Where were you last August when the A level results*
   were published?

This is the first of a few less obvious questions. If the answer
is, 'On holiday in France', ask who was at the school to
deal with the many queries and problems that are bound to
arise when exam results are published. I think the head ought
to be there. Last year I was at a girls state school when the
GCSE results arrived during the holidays. The headmistress
and several members of staff were there to receive the results
and to congratulate, console and advise the many girls who
came in to find out how they had fared. That is the kind
of commitment that gives teachers the right to be called
professionals. It also tells you more about the school's attitude to the pupils than all those statements in the prospectus
about the school being a family.

12 *How do you prevent stealing by pupils?*

Stealing is seldom mentioned in the school rules. Is that
because everyone knows stealing is wrong or because schools
are reluctant to acknowledge that stealing is a problem? I
doubt whether there is a secondary school in the country that
does not experience stealing by pupils from pupils, if not constantly, then as a recurring incident. It appears to make no
difference whether the pupils are privileged or disadvantaged.
Money in particular is stolen, mostly I suspect on an oppor-
tunistic basis, but sometimes as a premeditated crime. Stealing
is often linked to illegal drugs and also to bullying, when older
pupils 'borrow' money and refuse to pay it back. So what is
the head doing to combat this? The honest answer is that there
is little a headmaster can do, except make his own position
clear by the way he deals with thieves and talks about the case
to the school assembly, and by encouraging pupils to be more
alert in protecting their own property. The dishonest answer
is that it is not really a problem.

13 *How many pupils did you expel last year and for what reasons?*

This is a double-check question. You want to know where the school draws the line and confirm whether this is consistent with what the head has been telling you about discipline. Don't expect the head to know the answer off the cuff; he does not keep the score on the study wall. The total is likely to be three or four expulsions a year, regardless of the size of the school. It is as if heads have agreed that this number represents a sensible compromise between maintaining discipline and avoiding bad publicity. Is the tough stance the head claims to adopt on illegal drugs and bullying reflected in the reasons for expulsion?

14 *Are you currently applying for other jobs?*

If your children are not due to enter a school for the next two to three years, you have a legitimate interest in knowing whether there is going to be a change of head. Parents usually put the question more tactfully: Do you have any plans to move on? Or, more flatteringly, You're not thinking of leaving are you?

There is nothing you can do about changes at the top, but knowing that change is likely to occur might help to clarify your decision about a school. But the secondary purpose of the question is to encourage the headmaster to talk less defensively about the job. By focusing on his future rather than the school's, you should unlock some of the true feelings behind the official answers. You don't expect him to share confidences with you about how he gets on with the governors or the staff, but implicit in his thoughts about his own future will be his awareness of what still needs to be done and whether he is the man to do it.

Leading on from this, you could also ask whether there is an ideal time for a head to stay at one school. A head probably does his best work for the school somewhere between his third and tenth year. If he is applying for another job after two years, something is wrong with him or the school. After ten years he should be thinking about leaving, but many heads stay put because they know it is difficult to find another job. After fifteen years, the virtues of the best heads may become liabilities. There are exceptions to all these rules but I think I would deliberately avoid sending a child to a school where a long-serving head was about to retire. His successor will have a hard task, which may last several years, repairing the damage inflicted by a predecessor who stayed too long.

Even the most accommodating head will not be able to give you enough time to ask all these questions. Select the ones you want to put to the head personally; others can be put in writing either before or after your visit. I need hardly remind you that some schools will abstain from this type of correspondence with prospective parents, that some heads will refuse to be pinned down to a question-and-answer session and that those heads who are generous with their time may be economical with the truth.

Yours sincerely
John Rae

15 Is it necessary to check out a school's governors? How important are they?

Dear Alyce

It is worthwhile trying to find out how the governors operate, in particular their working relationship with the head. *Who* the governors are is less important.

You should not assume that titles and ranks on the governing body are a guarantee that a school will be well managed. The aristocrat, the general and the bishop may or may not be good governors, but their presence tells you nothing about the quality of the school. A superficially impressive list of governors has not prevented independent schools falling on hard times, nor has it ensured that crises are well handled.

I do not believe that there is any magic combination of expertise which constitutes the ideal governing body, but I would be interested to know the ages and occupations of the members. As far as I know, no school publishes this information, but I would have thought it was information that parents should have. The inept handling of recent crises in independent schools, such as Dulwich and Cheltenham, over the dismissal of the headmaster surely owed something to the fact that parents and governors knew so little about each other.

I would be reassured if one governor had experience of running a good school (but one is enough, you do not want the governing body to be cluttered with former headteachers). As for the rest, what matters is that governors should be men and women of the world and not local busybodies. State school heads will protest that local governors are not busybodies; they are men and women who are prepared to give their time and expertise to serve on the governing body and its committees. But it is not the fact that the governors are local that I am critical of; in a state school and in many independent day schools they are bound to be. I am critical of an attitude of mind that the phrase 'local busybodies' implies: narrow in outlook and inclined to tell others how to do their job.

By 'men and women of the world', I mean those who have seen and done enough to have gained a certain degree of wisdom. They do not have to be worldly. A monk or a nun may be a man or woman of the world in the sense that matters to a school. Men and women of the world may have diverse virtues and vices, but they have one thing in common. They are not small-minded and that is what makes them so valuable as members of a governing body.

Too many retired people on the governing body are a liability. There is nothing more likely to sound the death knell for a struggling school in these competitive times than a governing body dominated by men and women with time on their hands. The temptation to interfere in the running of the school is almost irresistible.

Former pupils on the governing body are not necessarily a drag on progress. It depends on the school. A less-academic school is likely to have former pupils of limited intelligence whose presence on the governing body is not going to be conducive to inspired thinking about the school's future. But the leading independent schools can recruit from their alumni those men and women of the world whose wide contacts, sense of proportion and ability to think strategically are invaluable. Eton is governed almost exclusively by its old boys and I doubt whether there is a better-managed school anywhere.

State schools are required to include on their governing bodies governors elected by the parents and the teaching staff; independent schools are not. That difference is symptomatic of a different approach to the governors' role. In the state schools, the governing body represents the local community. Independent schools may have strong links with the local community, but they are not community schools. State school governors are governing the school on behalf of the local community; independent school governors are governing on behalf of the school itself.

I do not wish to exaggerate or simplify the difference this makes, but it would be broadly true that those who govern on behalf of the local community have both an obligation and a stronger motivation to participate in the management of the school. The school's admissions policy is the governors' policy, not the head's, and it is the governors who have to answer parents' criticisms when their report is presented to the annual parents meeting. In an independent school it is extremely rare for parents to have direct access to the governing body. It may be argued that easy access to state school governors – whose addresses are often published in the prospectus – makes them a target for trivial or malicious complaints, but it is also true that the inaccessibility of independent school governors can allow heads to get away with incompetence or worse.

It is particularly interesting to see how governors operate in grant-maintained schools which have opted out of local education authority control. Because they have much greater independence, you would expect the governors to act in a similar fashion to those in an independent school. In one sense they do: they take on the strategic role that used to be played by the local education authority. But in another sense they do not. They are involved in more decision making about policy than would be normal in an independent school. Heads of grant-maintained schools seem undecided whether this means the governors are now more 'interventionist' or more 'supportive'.

Though there are differences in the governors' role, the heads of state and independent schools would probably have little difficulty agreeing where the line should be drawn between the governing body's responsibilities and the head's. It is against their view of what is best practice that I suggest you measure any information you can obtain about the way a governing body operates.

It is not the governors' job to run the school; they employ the head to run the school for them. The governors monitor the performance of the school and hold the head accountable; the head and the senior staff management team must have control of operational matters. The governors are involved in strategic not detailed planning; their detachment enables them to see the head's proposals in the context of the overall direction for the school and the development plan that has been agreed. The governors have an overseeing role; they do not have the time, or the expertise, to engage in hands-on management.

It sounds straightforward but misunderstandings and conflict are commonplace in both state and independent schools. There is nothing new about this. The great, pioneering Victorian headmasters such as Thomas Arnold of Rugby and Edward Thring of Uppingham fought fierce battles to ensure that the trustees did not interfere in the running of their schools. Thring, in particular, was constantly at loggerheads with his trustees, describing them as a 'cold and hostile phalanx' opposed to everything he wished to do.

It is largely thanks to the battles Arnold and Thring fought that independent school heads have been able to enjoy greater freedom than their state school colleagues. Now, however, that greater freedom is in danger of being eroded as the market in independent education gets tougher. State school heads, too, are under pressure from their governing body to deliver success and this pressure, combined with the requirements of new legislation – such as the Children Act 1989 – has made governors in both state and independent schools more reluctant to stay their side of the line.

So, while conflict between the head and the governors is nothing new, my guess is that it is becoming more frequent; at least in the independent sector, which has set up a 'flying squad' of experienced governors to visit schools in trouble and help mend fences between the head and the governing body. That is why the questions raised in your letter are important and why I suggest you should at least try to find out how the governors operate.

The key relationship is between the head and the chairman of the governing body. If these two trust and understand one another, the potential for conflict will not be damaging to the school. Some tension between head and governors is not only inevitable, it is desirable. There would be something wrong with a school where there was no tension between the head's ambitious plans and the governors' caution. Like a strong dog taking its owner for a country walk, the head should set the pace while the governors retain the ultimate authority. If the roles are reversed, with the governors setting the pace and the head following behind, the creative tension is lost, along with the head's credibility, particularly in the eyes of his staff.

It is the chairman's job to manage the tension between the head and the other governors. He must encourage the head to take the initiative, while reassuring his fellow governors that the head's plans are subject to their approval. He must also ensure that the governors understand the difference between taking an active interest in the school and interfering in day-to-day operations. Most difficult of all, he has to distinguish between well-founded criticisms of the head and deliberate attempts to stir up trouble. It may surprise you to learn that there are governors who appear to relish stirring up trouble for the head. Perhaps they love intrigue. Perhaps the head has asked for it through his ill-disguised impatience at having to submit his plans to the governing body. All heads make enemies; it is in the nature of the role. But as long as the head and the chairman stand together, the troublemakers are kept at bay.

Unless parents are well tuned in to the local gossip, or have first hand experience of how schools work, they will be unaware of the various conflicts that may be going on behind the show of unity on the speech day platform. As prospective parents you wish to know whether the school is effectively managed, so it makes sense to ask about relations between the governors and the head. The best source of information is the head himself, unless you happen to know one of the governors well. 'How do you get on with the governors?' is rather too blunt, but you could ask the head how much interest the governors take in the school. As is so often the case with questions to the head, it is not so much the factual information you are seeking but the truth behind the answer.

I think you will be able to tell from the way the head speaks about the governors whether there is a good working relationship. Because the head's emotions are engaged in a way they are not when he is speaking about exam results or building plans, he will find it difficult to disguise his true feelings. What you are looking for is not an assurance that all is sweetness and light in his relations with the governing body, but some indication that the inevitable tensions are being resolved in a way which benefits the school and that he is pulling the governors forward, not following obediently in their footsteps.

Yours sincerely
John Rae

16 What are the effects of different class sizes on pupils?

Dear Siobhan

Politicians are being disingenuous when they say there is no research evidence to show that small classes produce better results. We do not know exactly how class size is related to academic achievement because there are other factors at work, such as the quality of the teaching and the general level of discipline. But just because we are unable to separate class size from the other factors does not mean that class size makes no difference.

Politicians are on stronger ground though when they point to countries where large classes are not incompatible with effective learning. In Japan, classes in primary schools are commonly forty to forty-five pupils and the Japanese teachers are very successful at instilling basic skills and knowledge with that age group. But their success depends on a culture of order and a style of teaching which are alien in Western societies, such as our own or the United States. We could improve our classroom control, but we cannot borrow Japanese culture.

The Japanese experience does emphasize, however, that class size is not *in itself* the key to whether children learn or not. It is the combination of manageable size, with good teaching and good discipline that matters. Independent preparatory schools in this country believe a class is becoming unmanageable if it is larger than twenty and at many of these schools the average class size is twelve. In state primary schools, class sizes of more than thirty are common. Our four-year-old granddaughter will either go to the nearest state primary school where her class will have forty-one pupils, or to the nearest independent school where her class will have ten. No wonder governments are so anxious to reassure parents that class size does not matter.

At the secondary level, the difference between the independent and state schools is less marked. There are a handful of independent secondary schools where classes are never larger than twelve, but generally boys and girls taking GCSE will be in classes of about twenty-five pupils, compared with state school classes at that level of about thirty. When there are sets for options, such as a second language, the size of the set is likely to be similar in both types of school. In the sixth form, the independent schools may have larger groups because more pupils stay on to do A level.

It is at the all-important first stage of a child's education, therefore, that pupils in independent schools enjoy the advantage of smaller classes. If you have limited funds to spend on education, the time to spend them is when your children are young. But you should not assume that the local primary school has more than thirty in a class, because the size varies from one local education authority to another. Nor should you mistake the published staff-pupil ratio at an independent school for the average class size. It is the latter you are interested in. In independent schools as a whole there are about ten or eleven pupils to every member of the teaching staff, but in many of these schools you will still find that the average class size below the sixth form is over twenty.

Some researchers have argued that twenty is the critical number: above twenty extra numbers in the class make little difference, but below twenty each reduction brings about a significant improvement in the pupils' performance. Experienced teachers know that if you drop the class size below twenty, the benefits for pupils and teachers go on increasing. Teaching fifteen really is different from teaching twenty. But

I doubt that they would agree that above twenty extra numbers make little difference to a pupil's education.

Consider three aspects of successful teaching: preparation and feedback, relations with pupils and classroom control. If you are preparing to teach a lesson on simultaneous equations, or on the causes of the Second World War, the size of the class does not make much difference. But when you collect their work, to mark and return the next day, the size of the class matters a great deal. Pupils learn by trial and error, a process in which the teacher's feedback plays a crucial role. In large classes a teacher does not have time to discuss with all the pupils individually where they have gone wrong and why.

Good teachers know their pupils. If you want a foolproof test of whether a school is worth sending your children to, walk into a classroom at random and ask the teacher to name all the pupils. An experienced teacher will have a technique for learning his or her pupil's names quickly, such as insisting they always sit in the same place, because he or she knows a relationship with each one of them must be established. Few things are more calculated to inhibit learning than the realization that the teacher does not know who you are. The larger the class, the greater the difficulty of establishing those vital relationships.

From the relationship between the teacher and the pupils stems the basis of good discipline. Your threats lack conviction if you cannot remember the culprit's name. But if the pupils know that you are interested in them as individuals, it does not matter whether they like you or not, or whether they like your subject or not, you have the essential precondition for keeping them under control. It requires a gifted teacher to achieve this balance with a large class.

Class size is one of those subjects on which I prefer to trust the instinct of parents and the experience of teachers than the findings of research. Whether there is an ideal class size at each level, I do not know. The manageable size is the number of pupils a good teacher can teach, know and control effectively.

I would have thought that an A level class above fifteen, a GCSE class above twenty-five and a primary or preparatory school class above twenty were in danger of becoming unmanageable.

I do not mean to imply that good teachers cannot manage larger classes – they do so successfully in many state primary schools – but I am suggesting that you use these observations as a rough guide when you are visiting schools.

Class size does matter. What amazes me is that anyone should doubt it.

Yours sincerely
John Rae

17 How do teachers in independent schools compare with teachers in state schools?

Dear Juliet

I am wary about responding because this area is a minefield and I fear I shall tread so carefully, you will learn nothing you did not know already. The cautious answer is that there are good teachers in both types of school and bad ones too. But what parents want to know is whether the teachers in independent schools are better at their job than teachers in state schools. If they are not, one of the principal reasons for paying fees is removed.

No one is keen to address this question. The heads of independent schools have no hesitation in saying that their schools have better facilities and smaller classes, but they will not say that they have better teachers. Most of them offer more generous salaries for the specific purpose of attracting the better teachers, but public comparisons between their own staff and teachers in state schools are taboo.

There are a number of reasons for this. Everyone knows from their own experience that some teachers are better than others, yet the teaching profession is very reluctant to see this obvious fact given any public recognition. Although there is little solidarity between teachers in independent schools and teachers in state schools – many of the former will have nothing to do with teachers' unions – on this question there is enough fellow feeling to deter one group from commenting on the performance of the other. In addition, there is the difficulty of comparing the teachers' task in different situations. How do you compare the skills needed to interest a large group of slow learners, with those required to interest a small group of Winchester scholars?

This reticence does not help parents. They know that teachers in different types of school may face different problems, in and out of the classroom, but they believe there must be some way of deciding whether one teacher is better than another and whether the better teachers are more likely to be found in independent schools.

Qualifications do not make a better teacher, but they are a good place to start. All but a few teachers in independent secondary schools have a degree in the subject they teach. The same is true of state secondary schools with flourishing sixth forms. In other comprehensives key subjects, such as science and mathematics, may be taught by people without a degree in *that* subject. It is true that at some public schools, classics masters used to teach English and form subjects, but mathematics and science are a different matter and the absence of properly qualified teachers in these subjects must place some state school pupils at a disadvantage.

Using this definition of what it means to be qualified, there is likely to be a higher concentration of 'better teachers' in independent schools. But if you define a qualified teacher as someone who has a degree or postgraduate qualification in education, then you will find a higher concentration in state schools. Bachelor of Education degrees are rare in independent schools (except, curiously, among physical education staff) and although most teachers in independent schools now have a postgraduate certificate of education, this qualification is not thought by the schools to have much bearing on whether the individual will make a good teacher. A teaching qualification as distinct from a degree in the subject you teach is essential for those in state schools, but not for those in independent schools. State school teachers are also more likely to value in-service training, to join a union and to take an active interest in the ideological and political debates surrounding education.

Those who choose to teach in independent schools tend to opt out of the ideological and political debates, except where they directly affect the future of the schools in which they are working. You will not find staff in an independent school common room arguing over whether streaming and whole-class teaching should be re-introduced, because they never abandoned them in the first place. If independent schools sometimes seem like neutral countries in a world at war, it is not surprising that they attract men and women who are more interested in their specialist subject than in the theory and politics of education, and who are more in sympathy with traditional teaching methods.

But it would be wrong to stress this comparison too strongly. There are many traditional, apolitical teachers in state schools, particularly in those that have retained something of the grammar-school ethos. The contrast is really between two types of teacher rather than between teachers in two types of school. It is the difference between teachers who are in their job because they are genuinely interested in the young and want to help them to learn, and teachers who are in the job for any number of other reasons. It is the former who will always be the better teachers. Not even an interest in their subject, which is important enough, is as vital as an interest in the pupils they teach; and no first-class degree or firm grasp of educational theory can compensate for its absence.

Some men and women are born teachers, or so it seems. The enjoyment of young people's company and the impulse to teach is in their nature. Other good teachers have surprised themselves in their vocation. They had not thought of teaching, not at school level anyway, and they came to it as a second- or third-choice career, but against their expectations, they too enjoy the company of the young and find that it is their interest in their pupils and their progress that makes the job worthwhile.

A teacher who is primarily motivated by a desire to change

society – who sees the classroom as a means to this end – will never be a good teacher because he is pursuing his own agenda, not his pupils'. There are some politically-motivated teachers in state schools, but most teachers in both types of schools are pragmatic in their approach to education. Different teaching methods and varied ways of organizing the school are not political issues, but practical ones. The underlying issue is that whatever promotes effective learning is undoubtedly the best policy.

Good teachers are bound by a common interest in their pupils. I would also expect them to have in common an enthusiasm for their subject, a sense of humour so that they do not take themselves too seriously and sufficient stamina to outlast the most demanding pupils. But, in the other aspects of their personalities, in their talents and interests, good teachers follow no obvious pattern. Indeed, it is their very diversity which makes the school work for the pupils. One of the most intriguing aspects of education is the way in which different pupils find different teachers sympathetic or unsympathetic, inspiring or dull. Some good teachers are universally admired, but others have a divisive effect provoking strong, but contrary, feelings within the same class. Heads prefer the former but there is no doubt that the latter, however difficult for the head to handle, may inspire a pupil's love for that teacher's subject which lasts a lifetime.

It is sometimes argued that teachers in independent schools have an easier job than their counterparts in state schools. They almost always teach in more agreeable surroundings. They are paid more, though exact comparisons of pay scales are difficult. They seldom have to deal with seriously disruptive pupils and never with violent parents. Academic or social selection provides them with well-motivated pupils, while smaller groups and good school discipline make it easier to control the classroom.

But that is not the whole picture. In academically selective schools the pupils can be more demanding. A teacher who moved from a rural comprehensive school in Lincolnshire to an independent girls school in York told me that it took a year to adjust to pupils who challenged her at every turn. Anyone who thinks it is easy to control highly-intelligent adolescents has never tried. Those who teach in independent boarding schools have demands made on their time and energy that even a teacher in a tough, inner-city comprehensive would find it hard to cope with. Nor are independent school parents the unquestioning supporters state school teachers sometimes imagine; they may not resort to violence on speech day, but they are more litigious and interventionist now than at any time in the past.

At heart, it *is* the same job whatever the school, though the circumstances in which teachers have to work may be very different. There are some independent school teachers who could adapt to a state school without difficulty and vice versa, but there are others who could not begin to cope with the different environment. But that one environment might be more attractive than the other is suggested by the fact that three times as many state school teachers move to independent schools each year than the other way round.

I think there are factors which make it more likely that your children will encounter good teachers in the leading independent secondary schools, than in all but a few state schools. The leading independent schools have great advantages in the competitive market for the best teachers. When so few well-qualified candidates are available to teach subjects such as mathematics, science and modern languages, the wealthy, prestigious and academically-powerful school is bound to have an edge. And, although 'well-qualified' does not translate automatically into 'good teacher', these independent schools have a better chance of getting the best of both worlds – good teachers who are also well qualified to teach their subject.

I would be less confident that this was true at the junior level, that is to say that there are more likely to be good and well-qualified teachers in independent preparatory schools than in state primary schools. There are some very good independent preparatory schools, on which the leading senior boys' boarding schools in particular rely for their intake, but in recent years there has been a proliferation of independent day schools at the junior level, some of which are of doubtful quality. State primary schools, too, include some which are good – but of which little is heard – and others that are bad, which are taken as the norm. The bad press state primary schools occasionally receive seldom acknowledges the fact that many of the top academic independent schools actually recruit from state primary schools from the age of eleven. At the North London Collegiate School, the most successful academic girls' school in the country, half the eleven-year-old entry comes from state primary schools. At the academically successful state schools almost all the pupils come from this source. And, if you look further ahead, the majority of successful applicants to Oxford and Cambridge have been educated in state primary schools, whatever secondary school they subsequently attended. On these grounds alone it would be nonsense to suggest that your children are more likely to encounter good teachers in independent preparatory schools than in state primary schools. Everything would depend on which particular school you were talking about.

All heads try to build the best teaching staff available, but in practice this is similar to a card game in which you try to build a winning hand by releasing some cards and acquiring others. The perfect hand always eludes you and so do the perfect staff. In selecting good staff, the heads of independent schools have several advantages, in addition to being able to offer more competitive salaries. Unlike the heads of state schools they do not have to defer to the opinion of governors, who are not qualified to select teachers. Nor do they have to cope with the quick turnover of teachers. There is a general stability about the staff of most independent schools which must benefit their pupils.

The diplomatic answer to your question is that there are

good teachers in both independent and state schools and bad ones, too. The undiplomatic answer is that there is a higher proportion of good teachers in the leading independent second-ary schools than anywhere else; even the successful state schools have to operate under constraints that make appoint-ing staff more difficult. But state secondary schools which select pupils on an academic basis are likely to have a higher pro-portion of good teachers than the smaller, more remote inde-pendent boarding schools who are scraping the barrel when it comes to recruiting. State primary schools which feed academic secondary schools must have good teachers, as must the high-flying independent preparatory schools, but some private primary schools may employ too many unqualified teachers. Finally, inner-city state schools may tend to attract politically motivated teachers whose real interest is not in their pupils.

Yours sincerely
John Rae

18 What do contemporary boarding schools have to offer?

Dear Natasha and Mark

The shrinking market for boarding has not reduced the value of what boarding schools have to offer. On the contrary, it has stimulated the better schools to overhaul their operation and to pay more attention to the customer. So that while some boarding schools are in decline, adversity has made others a more attractive proposition.

Boarding schools offer a choice which is not, in fact, limited to those who can afford to pay the full boarding fee. There *are* boarding places in good state schools, for which you will have to pay less than half the cost of an independent boarding school. It is one of the best kept secrets of our state education system.

Boarding school heads say that the choice they offer is not a better education, but a fuller one. I cannot emphasize too strongly that this is true of good boarding schools, not of all of them. The extra time that good boarding schools use so well becomes a source of boredom and disaffection in bad ones.

No boarding school can assume that there will be a market for what it has to offer. There may still be valid reasons for sending a child to boarding school, but it is no longer an automatic choice for those who can afford to do so. The snobbery that once argued that day education, however excellent academically, was socially inferior to boarding education is no longer taken seriously. Most parents base their decisions on practical, not snobbish or sentimental, considerations. Only 7 per cent of parents with children at boarding school attended the same school themselves.

Disentangling parents' real motives for sending their children to boarding school is not easy. Some motives are straightforward. Parents working overseas, who want their children educated in Britain, account for one fifth of all boarders. Dissatisfaction with what is available in local schools, which have low academic standards and poor discipline, is another uncomplicated reason for choosing boarding. So is the pursuit of excellence in particular fields: for some children, boarding is the only way to obtain specialist music education. The pursuit of academic excellence may also be a practical consideration. For although we associate academic success with the highly-selective day schools, a glance at the A level league table shows that some less-selective boarding schools are equally successful. In the case of boarding places in state schools, the desire to give their children a better academic education is the reason most often given by parents for making this choice.

If some or all these motives are reinforced by a desire to choose a school where the other families broadly share your values, I see nothing wrong with that. There is no reason for middle-class parents to feel guilty if they want their children to be educated at predominantly middle-class schools. It happens the world over. Nor do I think parents should feel guilty if their motives appear to be selfish. If both parents are working long hours or frequently travelling on business, boarding school may provide a more secure base for education than home.

It is tempting to accuse boarding school parents of contracting out the task of bringing up their children; but even if the motives were that simple, there is no reason to believe that the task would be completed any more successfully than if the child stayed home and went to a day school. The family is the theatre in which most young people act out the rites of passage from childhood to adulthood, but boarding schools offer a legitimate alternative. The rebellious adolescent takes on the school rather than his parents, at least during term time. For two thirds of the year the school absorbs the strain. That may suit some adolescents as much as it suits their parents. At boarding school, the adolescent has the support of their peer group. The authority figures, usually the housemaster or house-mistress, may be in *loco parentis* but they are not emotionally involved, and there are always plenty of other staff around, so that it is an unlucky rebel who cannot find someone to act as a 'character witness'. I am not saying that even the best boarding school is a substitute for the family, only that for adolescents in particular boarding school may offer some advantages over day school.

Many parents who send their children to boarding school would argue that far from being selfish it is they who are making the sacrifice – not just financially but by giving up the joy of being with their children for a large part of the year – so that the children can have a good education. If you are thinking of boarding school for your two children, I would not spend too much time analysing your motives, but rather concentrate on what it is about boarding that might benefit the children more than day school.

The academic, musical and sporting excellence of some boarding schools is not in dispute, but the heads of day schools would challenge two claims: first, that boarding schools offer a fuller education and secondly, that boarding school pupils develop greater independence.

If you were able to spend a few days rather than an hour or two visiting a good boarding school, you would be in a better position to assess the concept of a fuller education. It boils down to three factors: time, the availability of staff and the provision of facilities. The activities which day schools have to squeeze into the lunch hour, or tack on to the end of afternoon school, the boarding school can spread throughout the day and over the weekend. Many boarding schools provide accommodation for the staff so that these men and women are available to help run activities long after the teachers at day schools have gone home. The facilities, particularly for sport, are likely to be much more extensive in a boarding school. It is the sheer variety of opportunities to discover what it is you have an aptitude for and to develop it to a high level that justifies the claim to provide a fuller education. In this respect, a good boarding school will beat a good day school every time.

I am less persuaded, however, by the claim that boarding schools develop in their pupils a greater independence. The principal lesson learnt by living in an institution is how to live in an institution, and institutional life is more likely to develop dependence than independence. Being away from parents at a young age may teach boys and girls to hide their feelings, to put up with other people at close quarters and to do without some of the comforts of home. That may add up to being more self-contained, even more self-reliant, but I am not sure it adds up to being more independent. Of course, it depends what you think independence is. If you define it as the ability to 'survive behind enemy lines', then boarding school could be a useful preparation. But if you think (as I do) that it means independence of mind and spirit, the maturity to be your own man or your own woman, and the courage to swim against the tide of popular opinion, then I do not see any connection between being a boarder and this sort of independence. Good schools encourage their pupils to think for themselves regardless of whether they are boarding or day.

Some of the claims made in favour of boarding schools are justified, others are not; the same is true of the charges made against them. Few British institutions have been the object of such persistent criticism – from Henry Fielding's celebrated judgement in the eighteenth century that 'public schools are the nurseries of all vice and immorality', to the allegations of snobbery, philistinism and bullying that characterized the liberal assault on boarding schools two centuries later. What today's parents would like to know is whether the heads' assurances that boarding schools have changed beyond all recognition should be taken at their face value. The prospectuses are so full of happy, smiling faces that parents may wonder what it is the schools are trying to hide.

On all those aspects of boarding that have worried parents and fuelled criticism over the years, the schools have changed, though whether they have changed out of all recognition is open to question. Corporal punishment has been abolished. The bleak conditions have been transformed. The gruesome food has been replaced by cafeterias that offer a wide choice of menus, including salad bars and vegetarian dishes. The tyranny of prefects is as rare as a homosexual scandal. The closed society, to which neither parents nor the outside world were welcome, has become an open society which encourages parents to visit and allows pupils to go home at exeats and leave weekends. It is no surprise that, apart from those who live overseas, the majority of parents now live within an hour's drive of the school.

Boarding is not what it used to be, but you should not expect it to be a home from home. Institutional life is always a life lived in public, however much the old dormitories are partitioned. Large boarding schools will always be the most difficult schools to keep control of and when they are out of control some of the old ills return. You can measure how much schools have changed by how well they cope with the inescapable problems of running residential institutions for adolescents.

One of the least publicized aspects of contemporary boarding schools is that some of them seem to be out of control on a regular basis. Occasional bouts of anarchy have been a characteristic of boarding school life for generations, but something is wrong when every Saturday evening is a disciplinary nightmare for the school authorities. The trouble arises because the contrast between what the boarders do when they are based at home and what they are allowed to do at school is greater than ever before. The more parents turn a blind eye to what happens at adolescent parties, the more difficult it is for boarding schools to hold the line on Saturday evenings. Letting boarders sleep away more often during the term is a way of reducing the incidence of lawlessness on the campus. 'Get drunk at home for a change,' is one of the unspoken justifications for the weekend exeat, at least as far as the senior pupils are concerned.

Some schools handle this problem better than others. You can hardly ask the head how much illicit drinking goes on at the weekend, but you should enquire as to what the rules and arrangements are for each age group on a Saturday evening.

You should ask also about the provision of counselling for pupils. The law now requires a boarding school to appoint a counsellor who is independent of the school's disciplinary structure and easily accessible to the pupils. You should expect the system to be on the following lines.

In a co-educational boarding school in the West Country the counsellor is a female psychotherapist who is available to the pupils four days a week. For the first hour she sees anyone who cares to drop in and for the rest of the day she sees pupils by appointment. Pupils are referred to her by the school doctor, by the pastoral staff or by older pupils who have benefited from her help. She told me that the boys sought her help more often than girls, and hearties more often than aesthetes. The subject of the consultation remains confidential, unless it reveals a health risk or a threat of suicide.

Boarding schools are still adjusting to the role of the counsellor, so it would be worth asking how the new pastoral provision dovetails with the old and whether there is any conflict between counsellor and housemasters or between counsellor and parents.

As the better boarding schools overhaul their operation to retain their share of the market, the way they handle Saturday evenings and the integration of the counsellor are just two examples of their professionalism, which is in marked contrast to the cosmetic attractions of the less good schools. In the latter, colour co-ordination in carpets and curtains may seem a great improvement on the living conditions of old, but they do not compensate for poor discipline and amateur pastoral care.

The main problem for parents who are considering boarding schools is that there is such a difference between the top-of-the-range schools and the rest (though there is little difference in the fees they charge); and the consequences of making the wrong choice are likely to be more serious than a wrong choice of day school.

A professional couple, both working full time in London, decided to send their son to boarding school and chose a middle-of-the-range school that looked all right on paper; there was a bishop and a former cabinet minister on the governing body. But the housemaster was weak and had curious habits, such as locking the study door when interviewing boys and punching young boys behind the knee when overtaking them in the corridor. New boys were routinely bullied despite complaints from parents.

The professional couple gradually realized that what their son was telling them was true and after two years they plucked up the courage to tackle the headmaster about it. He told them that their son was a known troublemaker who was trying to distract attention from his own misdemeanours. They took their son away and, having difficulty persuading another school to take him, placed him in a crammer nearer home. A year later the housemaster was arrested while importuning men in a public lavatory.

Here you have an example of some of the characteristics of a bad boarding school: a headmaster who refused to believe that anything was wrong; a housemaster who should never have been appointed; and governors who looked good on paper, but who knew as little about the life of the boys as the trustees of the workhouse in *Oliver Twist*.

The answer to your question is that good boarding schools

have much to offer: a secure base for growing up, an alternative setting for adolescence, excellence in particular fields – academic or otherwise – and a wide range of facilities and opportunities for the pupils to discover what it is that interests them most. Some children flourish in this environment in a way they would never have done in a day school. But bad boarding schools have little to offer except poor leadership, insufficient supervision, house staff who are incompetent or worse and a superficial social cachet. If you continue to be interested in the possibility of boarding for your children, the need to take time and trouble over your choice of school is paramount.

Changes in the pattern of boarding may affect your choice. As the market shrinks more schools recruit overseas. You need to distinguish between good schools that have a well-established policy of attracting pupils from other countries and weak schools that are filling beds. A rough guide to aid differentiation is that the former will have pupils from a large number of countries, while the latter will have a large number of pupils from one or two countries.

The shrinking market has also encouraged schools to be more flexible about the age of entry. You no longer have to send your children away at a tender age to ensure a good chance of entry to one of the leading boarding schools at thirteen. Only 20 per cent of boarders start at the age of eight or younger. A small but increasing number switch from day to boarding for the two A level years. Flexibility also extends to weekly boarding which was once strongly opposed by boarding school heads, but is now accepted by many as one of the options they may have to offer. About 10 per cent of boarders are weekly boarders.

Such flexibility means you do not have to make a total commitment to boarding when your children are still young, but you do need to plan ahead. The more popular a school is, the less flexible it will be about age of entry. Flexibility may also have disadvantages. A school where pupils are coming and going as boarders may become more like a hostel and a school which mixes weekly boarders and full boarders is unlikely to be much fun for the latter.

The most striking feature of flexibility on the part of the boys' boarding schools (though headmistresses describe it as opportunism) is their admission of girls to the sixth form, or their conversion to full co-education. The traffic between the boys' and girls' boarding market has been almost entirely one way. There are eight thousand girls in what were boys' boarding schools, but less than two hundred boys in what were girls' boarding schools.

Headmistresses and parents may wonder how far the former boys' schools really have become co-educational, and you would be wise not to assume that every boarding school that advertises itself as co-educational is equally committed to the idea. Opportunism does not preclude making a success of co-education, but it takes time, at least five years, to adapt a long-established boys' boarding school to the demands of co-education, and I would be wary about sending a son or daughter to a school still in the process of transition. I would be wary, too, of a head who told me that the motive for change was educational. Market forces dictated the change, not just a shortage of boy boarders but parental demand for what they thought was a better education for their daughters. But the demand for co-education in independent schools may already have run its course and the conviction grows that single-sex education produces better academic results for boys as well as for girls, and that is one more reason for avoiding the recent converts to co-education.

The middle-class discovery of state schools which offer boarding is also a response to market forces. Such state schools charge for the boarding, but not for the tuition. At Reading School in Berkshire, for example, parents of boarders pay about £4,000 a year compared with £12,000 a year at an independent boarding school. When you see that Reading School's A level results are far better than those of most independent boarding schools you begin to realize what a bargain

it is. The disadvantage is that at Reading there are only a
hundred boarders in a school of seven hundred pupils and at
other similar state schools the proportion of boarders may be
even smaller. This does not mean that the boarders are not
properly looked after and provided for, but with one or two
exceptions the state schools that offer boarding facilities are
(for all intents and purposes) day schools with boarding units,
not boarding schools with remarkably low fees. It is not surprising then that the principal motive for choosing a state
boarding school is to give children access to a first-class academic education. If you are interested in state boarding, I suggest you contact the Boarding Schools Association which
publishes a *Directory of Maintained Boarding Schools*.

Many parents do not wish to consider boarding school for
their children; others know they will never be able to afford
it. But for those who are interested, there are some very good
boarding schools which are probably better at what they do
now than they have ever been, because competition to be one
of the survivors in the boarding market leaves no room for
complacency. What impresses me most when I visit these
schools is the sheer efficiency and professionalism of the organization. Boarding schools may have admirable mission statements and their heads may speak eloquently of the importance
of the individual, but it is efficient administration that contributes as much as anything to the welfare of the pupils. Nowhere
is the road to hell more likely to be paved with good intentions
than in a second-rate boarding school. My advice is to look
for efficiency and professionalism when choosing a boarding
school – they are the qualities that will stop bullying, not
declarations of concern. You are putting your children in their
hands and paying a large fee, so you should settle for nothing
less.

Yours sincerely
John Rae

19 Might the presence of foreign pupils in the school hold back our child's education?

Dear Mr and Mrs Davidson

That might happen if too many foreign pupils have been recruited from overseas to fill empty beds. It might also happen in an urban day school if there are a large number of pupils who may live in this country, but for whom English is a foreign or second language.

On the other hand, I think your child's education will surely benefit if the school's international dimension is the result of deliberate policy and not a shortage of pupils. But, be careful. The decline in the number of boarders has forced many independent schools into the international market and the heads have, understandably enough, decided to make a virtue of necessity. 'A commitment to international understanding' is not always what it seems.

One way of distinguishing the genuine article from the flag of convenience is the length of time the school's international dimension has been operating. Another is to ascertain whether the international dimension is an integral part of the school's life.

The international sixth form at Sevenoaks School, in Kent, is an example of the genuine article. It was started in the late fifties by the headmaster, Kim Taylor, who had taught overseas and believed in the educational advantages of an international sixth form. It was conviction not convenience, although Taylor's ideals did attract British parents who welcomed an alternative to the rather narrow horizons of the sixth forms in more traditional schools.

Taylor's governing body had doubts about the project, but did not wish to refuse a headmaster they had only just appointed. They did, however, insist that Taylor raise the money required for building and scholarships himself, which he did successfully from multi-national companies. The international sixth form now attracts about forty pupils a year from overseas, mostly from continental Europe. Although they represent only 20 per cent of the school's sixth form, the school offers to both home-based and overseas pupils the opportunity to study for the International Baccalaureate as an alternative to A levels. That is a genuine commitment to international education.

Another example is the group of twenty-two independent schools in nine countries known as the Round Square schools. Seven of these schools, including Gordonstoun, Cobham Hall and Abbotsholme are in Britain. What distinguishes these schools from the bed-fillers is that the international dimension is built in to the school's philosophy and organization. Every year the heads, staff, pupils and governors of Round Square schools meet, in one of the nine countries involved, to develop a mutual understanding rooted in some depth and to plan 'International Service' projects which pupils will undertake in the developing world.

The extent to which individual Round Square schools are international varies and I think it would be fair to say that the pursuit of academic excellence is not their priority, but the presence of foreign pupils in these schools is a bonus for the home-based pupils, not a burden.

The number of foreign pupils in Britain's independent schools continues to rise and stands at about 20,000. Although this represents less than 5 per cent of the total, foreign pupils tend to be concentrated in the weaker schools. When the Independent Schools Information Service (ISIS) reports that what overseas recruits are looking for is 'high standards and academic rigour', I cannot help admiring their nerve, because it is largely the absence of these qualities which caused the weaker schools to have empty beds in the first place.

Russian parents are the latest to discover the virtues of our independent schools. Recently, when I was visiting a small independent school in the West Country, the head introduced me to Sergei, a thirteen-year-old boy from Moscow. What on earth was Sergei doing in this undistinguished school in a sleepy English market town? The headmaster had been on a recruiting trip to Moscow and was proud of his catch. Maybe Sergei will benefit; maybe his English contemporaries will too. But the claim by ISIS that the 'benefit to Britain of establishing close links with future generations of well-educated foreigners who will assume influential positions in their own countries is inestimable' should be taken with a pinch of salt.

Your concern is whether Sergei and his fellow students from Eastern Europe, Hong Kong, Taiwan (to name only the main sources) should be taken into account when you are choosing a school. Quite apart from the possibility that your child's education might be held back, there must be a point at which the number of foreign pupils changes the overall nature of the school. A Christian foundation which falls over backwards to accommodate other faiths must lose something of its essential character without making any *real* gain in religious tolerance. Where this point of change is, I can only speculate. Between 10 per cent and 15 per cent of the year group from overseas might be the most a school can assimilate without becoming an uneasy hybrid, neither true to itself nor truly international. Schools like Ardingly, in Sussex, that suggest in their prospectus that they have the best of both worlds are not convincing. 'Ardingly is a Christian foundation and our four main Sunday chapel services a term are important occasions. It is also a very international school which has particularly strong links with countries in Europe and the Far East.'

There is another consideration. Even a smaller number of foreign pupils should sound a warning to parents. A school that has no choice but to recruit pupils from overseas is, by definition, struggling in the home market. That may be for reasons outside its control, such as geographical location, but whatever the reason the school is vulnerable. The flow of pupils from Hong Kong may not continue much beyond 1997, while the boom in applications from the former Soviet Bloc could well prove short-lived. Schools that are vulnerable to such changes have an uncertain future and it is probably wise to avoid them.

They may be particularly vulnerable if they are relying on short courses for overseas pupils who wish to improve their English. An International Study Centre offering an intensive one-year course in written and spoken English may help to balance the books at a remote independent boarding school, but is unlikely to provide long-term security.

A better bet for these schools would be to follow Sevenoaks' example and offer the International Baccalaureate (IB) alongside A levels. A state school in rural Wales has decided to respond in that way to the problem of falling roles. Whether Ysgol Y Preseli in Dyfed will obtain the European money it needs to set up the residential IB course for overseas pupils, which will also encourage its own pupils to stay on in the sixth form, remains to be seen. But it is taking the challenge of opening its doors to international pupils seriously which is more than you can say for most independent schools.

You should worry if the school you are considering is dependent on foreign pupils for its financial viability. That is not always easy to judge. Look out for a prominent reference to international airports in the prospectus and ask the head if he goes on recruiting trips abroad. Successful boarding schools receive several unsolicited applications from foreign pupils every week; regular recruiting trips should arouse your suspicion. The head may be inclined to play down their significance and to be evasive about the exact number of foreign pupils in the school. I like the honesty of Cranleigh School, in Surrey, which in a series of pie charts shows parents exactly how many overseas pupils there are and which countries they come from. I conclude from its honesty that it has found a way to accommodate – in both senses – the foreign pupils without holding back the standard of education for the others.

In an urban day school, you should worry if pupils who do not have English as their mother tongue are holding back the education of those who do. You will find the heads of state schools just as glib as their independent school colleagues when it comes to making a virtue of necessity. The benefits of being educated in a multi-cultural school spring all too easily to their lips.

You should not worry if a school appears to be too exclusively English. Appearances are deceptive; many of the leading independent schools are international under the skin. They do not have to recruit overseas, but their fame allows them to pick and choose the most talented foreigners. Eton draws pupils from many countries and offers international sixth form scholarships; St Paul's and Westminster attract the children of foreign diplomats and bankers living in London.

It comes down to this. What you are looking for is a school that will bring out the best in your child. Foreign pupils are likely to enrich your child's education if they are there on merit, or as part of a genuine programme to increase international understanding. Otherwise, they *may* hold back your child's education if they are there in significant numbers just to fill empty beds, or because the school serves a catchment area in which too many pupils are struggling with the English language.

Yours sincerely
John Rae

Part Three

ASSESSING THE NON-ACADEMIC ASPECTS OF A SCHOOL

20 Should we be worried if a good school has a reputation for being permissive about illegal drugs?

Dear Dr and Mrs Llewellyn

We corresponded before about the element of chance in education. The problem of illegal drugs is a good example of how your choice of school can load the dice in your children's favour.

We cannot blame all our children's mistakes on their peers, or protect them from all the ills of contemporary society. But neither do we have to leave it to chance. Who their peers are and who they will be pressurized by will partly depend on which school they go to. I am not forgetting also that the extent to which they are influenced will itself reflect on their personality and their upbringing, but as you have asked the question specifically about illegal drugs in the context of school, I would like to concentrate on what difference your choice of school can make.

The school you mention cannot be a good school, whatever its other achievements, if it really does adopt a permissive attitude towards illegal drugs. But I wonder whether that reputation is justified. In the Seventies and Eighties some schools ignored the problem because they did not wish to attract undue attention by expelling pupils. It was one of the ironies of the drug scene, particularly in relation to independent schools, that heads who refused to turn a blind eye received the worst publicity.

Today's parents are better informed and do not jump to the immediate conclusion that a school which introduces testing for illegal drugs must have a serious drug problem. Schools are better informed, too, and it is highly unlikely that *any* independent or state school now takes a lenient line on illegal drugs. However, it does not follow that they are all capable of handling the problem well. There are still a wide variety of responses and while none may be permissive, some are much more effective than others.

Judging the effectiveness of a school's response is not easy. The first step is to have as clear a picture as possible of the extent of drug use by young people in this country. It is just as important not to exaggerate the problem as it is to avoid complacency. Some people have a vested interest in embellishing the facts; if you can persuade society that everyone is smoking cannabis, for example, it is easier to argue for decriminalization. People whose livelihood depends on there being a problem to be tackled may also be tempted to overstate the case. Journalists, too, may hype a story or be selective in their use of the latest survey or research findings.

Even those who carry out the surveys and research may have their own agenda and may omit to point out that all estimates based on young people's self-reporting of an illegal activity are inherently unreliable.

'When older children and teenagers are using drugs,' reads one press report, 'children of six and seven can easily get involved in sniffing solvents and progress to smoking cannabis at eight or nine. By eleven they may be experimenting with LSD and Ecstasy.'

Compare that with the information from a more authoritative source, the British Crime Survey, that only 3 per cent of twelve- and thirteen-year-olds have ever taken an illegal drug. The press report implies that there is an easy and natural progression from solvents to cannabis to LSD and all before your child has left primary school. But there is no natural progression and while solvent abuse poses a serious risk for younger school children, the use of cannabis or LSD by children of primary school age would be extremely rare.

By the time they are sixteen, about 25 per cent will have smoked cannabis, though not on a regular basis. The figure for those who have ever tried any illegal drug is said to be about 30 per cent and may well be higher. The number of sixteen-year-olds who are *regular* users of illegal drugs – and this, I think, is the key figure – is estimated to be about 20 per cent.

These figures are probably conservative and they are always a year or two out of date. Local surveys in urban areas report higher figures. Nevertheless, it is clear that the *majority* of adolescents either do not use illegal drugs at all, or do so on an irregular, occasional basis. That in itself is not a cause for complacency, but neither does it justify the argument that we have to accept the 'normalization of drugs' among today's young people. If they think illegal drug use is normal, it is in the sense that they regard it as part of contemporary life, not in the sense that they are all partaking.

Although many young people appear to be able to steer clear of regular drug use, all young people are at risk. The availability of illegal drugs is deemed normal, even if regular use is not. Illegal drugs are available in rural schools as well as urban ones, to academic high fliers as well as slow learners, in affluent communities as well as disadvantaged ones, to girls as well as to boys. But the degree to which they are obtainable varies. In a school that handles the problem well, your children will be less at risk, regardless of where the school is situated and the type of community it serves.

The next step towards an assessment of a school's policy is to study two documents, both of which are available to parents. The first is a Department for Education circular of 1995 called *Drug Prevention and Schools*; it can be obtained from the Department's School Curriculum Branch in London. The second is the *Report of Drugs Guidelines Working Group* written by members of the Headmasters' and Headmistresses'

Conference in 1995 and available from the HMC offices in Leicester. The first is designed for state schools, both primary and secondary, and deals with tobacco and alcohol as well as illegal drugs. The second is designed for independent secondary schools and deals only with illegal drugs.

My reason for recommending these two documents is that they will, for the forseeable future, form the basis of schools' policies on illegal drugs. There are bound to be variations in the way different schools interpret the guidelines and implement the policy, so your choice of school will still be an important factor in your children's chances of steering clear of regular drug use. But the two documents will give you a yardstick by which a school's policy can be judged.

I recommend you concentrate on the following aspects:

1 *Is the policy written down and made available to prospective parents?*

The chances of finding any reference to illegal drugs in the prospectus are small, so you will need to ask for a copy of the school's policy. There is no statutory obligation for schools to have such a policy, but as prospective parents you have a right to know in some detail what the school's attitude is. Either the school will make its policy available to you in writing, or the head will explain it to you when you meet. If the school is unable or unwilling to tell you what its policy is, you should not send your children to that school.

2 *What provision is made for drug education?*

Health education in schools is a hit-and-miss affair. Whether it has any effect on the pupils' behaviour at the time, or later when they become adults, is uncertain. We hope that it does and that the effects are beneficial, but it would be a mistake to put too much faith in health education as an efficient deterrent to illegal drug use.

The effectiveness of health education can be undermined by a confusion of aims. Is the aim to discourage all illegal drug use or to help the young people 'manage' the risk? I think it should be prevention, but some schools regard 'management' as the only realistic option. By 'management' they mean ensuring the pupils have all the information they need to make considered decisions about the use of illegal drugs. The danger in this approach is that it tends to be neutral: 'we will give you the information, but we will not tell you whether we think taking illegal drugs is right or wrong'.

The young *do* have to make their own decisions, but they do not make them in a vacuum. The opinions of adults, especially of parents and teachers, are part of the context in which the decisions are made. If adults are neutral, the context is incomplete. The young may reject the teachers' views, but they have a right to know what they are and to either accept or reject their guidance.

Drug education is also more likely to be effective if it is part of a fully-developed health education programme, not a special topic that comes out of the blue. In the past, some independent schools thought they had dealt sufficiently with the issue of illegal drugs by inviting a visiting speaker to issue dire warnings to fifth year pupils. State schools are now required to deal with drugs at all the key stages of the National Curriculum, that is from the age of five to sixteen. Most independent schools would say that they do at least as much, but I have an impression that some still place too much confidence in shock-horror tactics and the visiting speaker. It would be worth checking. A talk given by a reformed drug addict is not a policy.

3 *How does the school deal with drug-related incidents?*

Good discipline is probably a more effective deterrent to the use of illegal drugs in schools than health education, but I doubt whether there is any other subject on which the head finds it so difficult to decide what the disciplinary procedures should be. Do you expel pupils for *all* drug-related offences? Do you distinguish between what happens at school and away from school? Do you take the pupil's age into account? Do you call the police? Do you introduce urine testing for cases where you have reasonable cause to suspect drug use?

These are not only difficult decisions for the head. They are also the questions to which you would like an answer when you are trying to assess how seriously the school takes this problem.

I think automatic expulsion in all drug-related offences on school premises is probably the best policy, but some heads of independent and state schools, whose opinion I respect, think that schools should now have a more flexible response.

The justification for automatic expulsion is that the *law* has been broken, not just the school rules, and that any less-draconian policy puts other pupils at risk. They are at risk outside the school, depending on whose company they keep, but even that risk can be reduced by the school taking an unequivocal line. For some years at Westminster I tried to make the rule on illegal drugs apply at all times, and wherever the pupils might be, but it didn't work. The best the school can do about what happens at home is to explain to parents why it is taking this particular stance and ask for their support.

Parents are understandably ambivalent. They want the school to take a tough line on drugs with other people's children, but think their own deserve a second chance. They are in favour of draconian measures *and* flexibility. Who wouldn't be in the circumstances?

Parents who condone illegal drug use, or are openly critical at home of the school's policy are a more serious problem for the head. The former probably don't know that *they* are breaking the law if they allow a friend of their son or daughter to bring drugs into the house.

Automatic expulsion has disadvantages. It can make the

head more reluctant to act on suspicion. If you know your enquiries may lead to expulsion, you may be selective about which rumours you pursue. Too many expulsions still bring bad publicity. For boarding schools which are short of pupils, they may also constitute bad economics.

As an alternative to expulsion, some heads of state schools use exclusion for a period followed by counselling, at least for a first offence. Some heads of independent boarding schools have introduced testing of urine or hair for traces of narcotics, not on a random basis but when there are reasonable grounds for suspicion. Testing removes the need for the long and often inconclusive investigations of pupils suspected of using illegal drugs. These heads also believe that testing offers a way out of the dilemma of how to be seen to take illegal drug use seriously without resorting to automatic expulsion. Instead of expelling those who confess to taking drugs and imposing no punishment on those who tough it out, the head has the option of offering the pupil a second chance on the condition that he or she submits to a testing regime as an alternative to expulsion.

Neither state schools nor independent day schools are in favour of testing. They argue that testing in a day school would be an unacceptable invasion of their pupils' private social activities. It is also too soon to tell whether the boarding schools' more flexible approach based on testing reduces or increases the risk of pupils becoming involved in illegal drugs.

From your point of view as prospective parents, the schools to avoid are those that have not taken the trouble to develop an effective policy. You can usually identify them by the fact that they do not have anything written down, or by the fact that the school appears to be neutral, or by the fact that the head denies there is a problem while blustering about how ruthless he would be if anyone dared to bring drugs into the school. As for reputations, I would take them with a pinch of salt. A school's reputation for being tough on drugs may be as misleading as its reputation for being permissive. One of the few prospectuses that mentions drugs, says, 'The possession, use or even attempted use of drugs, at or away from the school would lead to immediate expulsion'. Does the head mean what he says or is he just sabre rattling? A threat of immediate expulsion for attempting to use drugs on holiday lacks credibility.

An effective drug policy will reduce the number of druggie contemporaries your children will encounter, either because they have been deterred or because they have been expelled. While it may be true that the chances of having such contemporaries is greater in an urban day school, country boarding is no guarantee that they will not appear in the same form or the same house. It is the effectiveness of the school's policy that counts.

It is still realistic for parents to hope that their children will have nothing to do with illegal drugs. I do not think you should abandon that hope, even though you know that you may have to settle for the more modest outcome that your children emerge safely into adulthood with their occasional, experimental drug-taking days behind them. Which school you send them to *will* make a difference; not the whole difference, but enough to persuade you that the school's drug policy should be an important factor in your choice.

Yours sincerely
John Rae

21 Does alcohol misuse cause a greater problem for schools than illegal drugs?

Dear Mr and Mrs Troy

Yes. Illegal drugs may cause more serious problems, not least because the pupils are breaking the law, but the number and variety of problems caused by alcohol misuse is greater. However, it is not true, as is sometimes suggested, that heads do not take alcohol misuse seriously and devote instead a disproportionate amount of their time and authority to illegal drugs. Heads are worried that their pupils may be drinking too much, too young, but they seem less sure of how to deal with this than with other disciplinary problems, including illegal drugs.

Alcohol is a psychoactive drug. It is a two-faced drug, giving pleasure and causing trouble, if not in equal proportions, then apparently with equal ease. That is why alcohol presents a more complex challenge for schools than other drugs, legal or illegal. Tobacco is always bad for your health; we may not succeed in persuading pupils not to smoke, but that is our aim (or would be if teachers were not so craven about being 'judgemental'). With illegal drugs, too, our aim is to prevent, to deter, to dissuade. But what should a school's aim be in the case of alcohol?

Schools' difficulties in framing a policy are not helped by the curious provisions of the law. The legal drinking age in this country is five, not eighteen as is popularly supposed. Eighteen is the age below which it is illegal to buy or be sold alcohol. It is perfectly legal for a five-year-old to walk down a high street drinking a bottle of whisky. But that is not, of course, what society wishes to see. It is assumed that between the ages of five and eighteen children will be taught by both parents and schools to drink sensibly and not excessively, so that when they are allowed to buy alcohol for themselves, they will treat this powerful drug with the respect it deserves.

It hardly amounts to a public policy but in some respects it works. The great majority of young people do grow up to use alcohol sensibly, drinking at or below a level that, in the cautious language of the Department of Health, 'will not accrue significant health risk'. The United Kingdom is not the heavy-drinking country you might think from reading the press or observing a city centre on a Friday night; it is not even in the top-twenty consuming nations.

But that is not the whole picture. A minority of young people grow up to be heavy or problematic drinkers, though how much their experience in adolescence contributes to this is uncertain. More significant from a school's point of view is the arbitrary route some adolescents take to arrive at a more or less sensible drinking adulthood. Adolescence is the haphazard season, but in Britain drinking too much as a rite of passage to manhood (in particular) gives the problems of adolescence an extra twist. The age at which these drunken rites occur appears to be falling. Government figures show that between 1990 and 1994 there was a marked increase in the number of school pupils aged eleven to fifteen who drank alcohol on a regular basis. That confirms my impression on visiting schools. When I spoke about alcohol to a group of thirteen- and four-teen-year-olds at a leading independent boarding school, the master in charge told me that very few of the 150 boys and girls present had not been in trouble of one sort or another in the last year as a result of misusing alcohol.

I do not think that that particular boarding school's experience is unusual, though at a day school the alcohol misuse would take place out of school hours and would be primarily a problem for parents to deal with. But the day school, like the boarding school, has to work out what its attitude to alcohol is and what guidance it is going to give to its pupils.

If schools do not always respond adequately to the problem of alcohol misuse it is partly because heads know less about alcohol than they think they do. It is the fashion at many boarding schools to allow the older pupils to drink at a school bar or, if they are over eighteen, at specified local pubs. The school sets a limit which is usually two pints of beer or cider. The heads believe that allowing a limited amount of drinking, as a privilege for senior pupils, prevents over-indulgence and discourages illicit drinking lower down the school.

This approach may cause fewer problems than trying to ban alcohol altogether, but only if the heads really know what they are doing. In a boarding school in the north of England, the school bar was open to seventeen- and eighteen-year-olds five evenings a week with a limit of two pints of beer or cider on any occasion. I asked the head what type of beer or cider was available and he told me that the choice was a matter for the social committee, made up of senior pupils. I then asked him if he realized that a pint of super-strength beer or cider at 8 per cent or 9 per cent alcohol by volume, which is what many seventeen- and eighteen-years-olds choose to drink, contained almost as much alcohol as five whiskies. The school's policy of moderate drinking to prevent over-indulgence allowed the senior pupils to drink the equivalent of ten whiskies every night, five nights a week. Fifty whiskies a week is heavy drinking by any standards and is double what the government regards as a safe level of consumption for adults.

Ignorance of alcohol strength and of the law relating to alcohol and young people is surprisingly widespread among heads. Schools are also likely to reflect parents' ambivalence about teenage drinking. When something goes wrong, parents are up in arms and ready to blame the schools for being permissive, the licensees for selling to under eighteens and the drinks companies for making alcohol attractive to the younger age groups. But the same parents turn a blind eye every weekend when they know their sixteen- and seventeen-year-olds are off to the pub.

While society's ambivalence makes it more difficult for heads to work out an effective policy, some schools do seem to ask for trouble. When pupils leave day schools at lunch time and come back merry, that is not primarily an alcohol problem but a failure of school discipline. Why does the school not stop them going out in the first place? Boarding schools may also make it easy for their senior pupils to drink too much. In a recent case, a boarder went to a pub in the local town to celebrate his eighteenth birthday. His school friends challenged him to drink eighteen pints, but he collapsed after consuming twelve and was taken to hospital. The school rules allowed eighteen-year-olds to go into the town on Saturday evening, on the condition that they visited only one pub and drank no more than two pints. The boy's parents accused the school of abdicating responsibility; the head retorted that young people's attitudes to alcohol were formed in the home.

It is commonplace to find parents and schools accusing one another of being too permissive on the subject of alcohol. Yet parents and schools should share the same aim. While respecting the wishes of those who do not wish to drink alcohol at all, the aim is to help young people grow up to be sensible in their use of alcohol and to ensure, as far as possible, that the learning process does not involve risk. It is not the school's job to teach abstinence, but neither should the school's attitude endorse the view that alcohol is necessary to make any social occasion go with a swing.

I do not think you should expect schools to have a document entitled 'Alcohol Policy', but I do think you should expect the head and the staff to have thought through how the different pieces – education, school rules, example of adults, social occasions – fit together. What you are looking for is consistency and a clear sense that the school knows what it is trying to achieve. Without going into too much detail, the following illustrates what I mean and might be helpful.

Most children have their first taste of alcohol at home with their parents between the ages of nine and eleven. Alcohol education should, therefore, start in the primary or preparatory school. In practice, many of these schools arrange for a community police officer to come in and talk about illegal drugs, but they give alcohol a miss. Alcohol education continues to be a low priority in secondary schools where heads think they have 'done alcohol' when they secure the services of a recovered alcoholic to talk to the pupils. The message of the ex-alcoholic may be well meant but it is also ambiguous: don't follow my example, but if you do, it is possible to recover.

Pupils may be shocked temporarily by the alcoholic's story, but they do not identify with him. They are much more aware of the drinking habits of the teaching staff. A bar in the staff common room which is open at the end of the morning, a posse of teachers heading for the pub at lunchtime, and alcohol on the teachers' breath in afternoon school are not consistent with setting an example on sensible drinking. Alcohol as something you enjoy at leisure rather than during the working day is a good model for those approaching adulthood; a teacher who is desperate for a pint of beer after a stressful morning is not.

The school rules, too, need to be consistent with the aim. If the school bar in a boarding school is too loosely controlled and the authorities turn a blind eye to under-age drinking in the town pubs on a Saturday night, the pupils will draw the conclusion that while the adults preach moderation they are not too worried about over-indulgence. As parents we realize that our young may have to learn by trial and error, but in the case of alcohol we do not expect the school to provide the opportunities.

You may think you detect a whiff of puritanism in all this. It is true that having worked for the alcohol industry, I would take a less relaxed view of alcohol if I returned to head-mastering. Heads should not treat alcohol as though it were an illegal drug, but they should position it in their own minds and in the minds of their pupils as something to be associated with home and leisure, not school and work.

In boarding schools, in particular, there is too much alcohol in circulation. There is no need to have alcohol available on every social occasion from the parents' evening to the cast party at the end of the school play. A boarding school head-master recently complained to me that alcohol advertising was largely responsible for thirteen- and fourteen-year-old girls and boys drinking too much at a school dance, but why was alcohol available to that age group? The fact that more young teenagers are drinking alcohol regularly is not a reason for the school to endorse the trend. As for day schools, I would have thought there was a good case for their being 'dry' like United States navy ships, and indeed some are.

I do not want schools to demonize alcohol, but for them to make a comparatively small shift away from the assumption that alcohol should be available to certain groups and on certain occasions. If, for example, the boarding school bar was only open on Saturday evenings and alcohol was not automatically available on social occasions and teachers accepted a self-denying ordinance that they would not drink during the working day, that shift of emphasis would be achieved.

When you are visiting a school and talking with the head, it is this question of where the emphasis is placed that is most revealing. If the head dwells on the difficulty of preventing young people drinking too much when alcohol is so all-pervasive in society, in other words if he blames everyone else but himself for his pupils' alcohol misuse, you can be pretty certain that the school has no clear and consistent approach. But if the head sees the school's role as emphasizing that al-cohol need not be all-pervasive, you are probably right to conclude that the school has thought through its approach and steers a sensible course between over-reacting and under-reacting to the pupils' attempts to come to terms with our favourite drug.

Yours sincerely
John Rae

22 Are there any schools that have succeeded in eliminating bullying?

Dear Mr and Mrs Macpherson

No. But there are schools that have succeeded in making it less likely that bullying will occur and more likely that it will be stopped quickly if it does.

All parents fear that their child will be bullied at school. It must always have been so since the first school opened. There is something very primitive about the emotion you feel when you hear your child has been bullied. No parents worth their salt have not fantasized about going into the school to tell the bully responsible for tormenting their child to stop or else. They know they cannot protect their children all the time and that their children have to learn to cope with the petty cruelties that are bound to occur when a large number of children are thrown together. What they expect of a school is that it will prevent individual children being singled out as the focus for these petty cruelties. 'Any pushing, hitting, kicking, threatening, teasing or name calling which happens often enough to make a child feel hurt, frightened, sad or lonely is bullying', is the definition in the anti-bullying code of an independent prep school for boys aged seven to thirteen.

That is a good description of the type of bullying that may happen in a prep school or primary school. It is hardly an adequate description of the kind of severe physical and mental bullying Flashman and his cronies practised on the younger boys at Rugby. Flashman would not last five minutes in an independent boarding school today. The bullying of junior pupils by senior pupils in boarding schools is now very rare. But it has not disappeared altogether. In an independent boarding school in Sussex, routine bullying of new boys, under the guise of initiation rites, was still going on in the early 1990s. The headmaster who stopped it made himself unpopular with the old boys and senior staff and soon left. His predecessor who had turned a blind eye for nearly twenty years is looked upon as one of the school's best headmasters. Incidentally, the school prides itself on its Christian ethos.

There are, happily, very few boarding schools where those senior boys would have got away with that sort of bullying. There has been a genuine change of culture in independent boarding schools whereby senior boys and girls see it as their responsibility to stop bullying, and have few inhibitions about reporting serious cases to the staff. The abuse of power by prefects is now also virtually unknown, not because human nature has changed but because senior boys and girls no longer want to exercise power over others; they see themselves as representing the pupils' views to the head (and sometimes vice versa), as channels of communications, not figures of authority.

I must not paint a picture of today's sixth formers as angels of mercy, but in relation to bullying they are more likely to be a force of good than the reverse. This is a factor which applies to the good day schools, whether state or independent, as well as to the boarding schools, but it is in the latter that the change of culture is most striking. Whether the same is true of those secondary schools where there is no sixth form, I am not sure, but if you are considering such a school for your children, it is worth making a point of asking whether the fifteen and sixteen year olds play a role in preventing and stopping bullying and, if so, how effective they are.

Although the culture of schools is more explicitly opposed to bullying than in the past, bullying of pupils by their contemporaries, or by those in the year above, still occurs in all types of school. It is difficult to assess the extent of bullying in your own school and even more difficult to get an accurate picture of bullying in general. Parents tend to think that schools are complacent and that heads underestimate the problem. A 1996 survey by the National Confederation of Parent Teacher Associations suggested that the proportion of pupils who experience bullying is much higher than the 10 per cent often claimed. As a parent, you have to assume that bullying is an inescapable hazard of school life below the sixth form and that your children's chances of not being bullied largely depend on the attitude and policies the school adopts.

The various forms bullying takes have not changed much over the years. It is perhaps more likely to involve money now than in the past. Even primary and preparatory school pupils have been known to run sophisticated protection rackets and may have few qualms about demanding money with menaces. Pupils who 'lose' their pocket-money are almost certainly paying the bullies off. But the underlying cause of bullying does not change. Children and adolescents are insecure; if a scapegoat for the group's insecurity can be found, so much the better. There may be a hundred and one reasons why a particular pupil is forced to play that role, but what it always comes down to is that he or she is perceived to be vulnerable. Whether it is picking on the individual in class or roughing up him or her on the way home, whether it is verbal or physical, the fact is that some pupils enjoy bullying and other pupils join in or stand aside because they are afraid of being bullied themselves.

The secret of reducing the risk of bullying is good discipline. I do not mean harsh discipline; I mean discipline that is based on the professional commitment of teachers. Good discipline maintains order, and order is crucial to the reduction of bullying. A school which cannot control its pupils will certainly not be able to control the bullies among them.

This obvious fact is sometimes overlooked by those who search for new ways to respond to an age-old problem. Whatever the psychological explanation for their cruelty, Flashman and his gang flourished because the teaching staff in an early nineteenth-century public school did not consider it their responsibility to supervise the boys' lives outside the classroom, or to organize out-of-school activities. If bullying flourishes in the playground of some primary schools or during the lunch hour at some comprehensive schools, or in a boarding house at an independent school, the reason is likely to be the same. Leaving children or adolescents to their own devices for too long is asking for trouble. While the teachers in the staff room earnestly debate the causes of bullying and leave the supervision of the pupils to someone else, the bullies go about their business because they have a free rein to do so.

Teachers are not able to supervise all the pupils all the time, nor can they ride shotgun for the vulnerable pupils on the bus home. But they can be more vigilant than they are in some schools and more willing to intervene when it should be obvious that one child is being singled out by the group.

No amount of psychological insight or anti-bullying codes will reduce the risk of bullying if the school's discipline is poor. From your point of view as a prospective parent, therefore, the first thing to find out is not whether the school has an anti-bullying policy, but whether the school's discipline is good. But you should expect there to be an anti-bullying code or policy, preferably published in the school and made available to parents. The purpose of the code is to reinforce the school's public stand against bullying, to concentrate the minds of teachers on the need to be vigilant, and to help teachers, pupils and parents to know what to do if they are aware that bullying is taking place. Pupils and parents are encouraged to inform the school authorities, anonymously if necessary. In boarding schools there is often a school counsellor (usually a psychotherapist) to whom pupils can turn in confidence and the number of Childline is advertised by every house telephone. In girls' boarding schools it is not uncommon to find a bully box. As one head comments, 'The bully box is situated discreetly so that girls, in total privacy, can put in a note to say what or who is troubling them.'

On the question of bullying, heads have deliberately set out to undermine the traditional school ethics. 'Do not think of this as telling tales', one school's code reassures the pupils, 'bullying is too important not to report.' Whether schools will be successful in making bullying a special case to which traditional pupils' rules do not apply, I do not know. If they are, it is more likely to be with the younger pupils; at adolescence, the old taboo against informing on your peers is still strong which is why the attitude of the sixth form is so important.

Some heads in the independent sector fear a published code will be a hostage to fortune, a gift to an increasingly litigious parent body. Whether or not the code is published, you should ask the head what he or she would do if a serious case of bullying came to light. Some schools are now adopting a 'no blame' approach which, instead of punishing the bully, attempts to reconcile bully and victim, sometimes through the good offices of what might be called 'a pupils' court'.

I am sceptical of the 'no blame' approach. In certain cases it is helpful to encourage the bully and the bullied to talk through what has happened and why; and there are times when the best way to stop bullying in class is to discuss the issue with the whole group without attempting to identify the ringleaders or to apportion blame. But, where there is a clear case of persistent bullying and clearly identifiable bullies, the latter should be punished, and in serious cases this should mean exclusion or expulsion from the school.

Schools will never eliminate bullying, but you can increase the chances of your children not being victims if you choose a school where the discipline is good. The signs that the head and the staff have lost control are not difficult to spot. Some day schools, for example, dare not have a proper lunch hour during which extra-curricular clubs and societies meet because they are afraid of what the pupils might get up to. Instead, they push on as quickly as possible with afternoon classes and finish the school day early. This isn't for the convenience of those with longer journeys; it is done because the staff have lost control. And schools that have lost control of the lunch hour have probably lost control of the classrooms as well. Bullying will go on under the nose of teachers who are unable or unwilling to prevent it.

I should think twice about sending your children to a school which has no written policy on bullying, or where the 'no blame' approach is too open ended to be a deterrent. I know of no evidence that bullying is more likely to occur in a large school than a small one – as long as the pastoral units are themselves small – in a boarding school rather than a day school, in a single-sex rather than a co-educational school, or in an independent rather than a state school. Bullying doesn't work that way. It moves in to occupy a pastoral or disciplinary vacuum wherever that appears.

Yours sincerely
John Rae

23 Do independent schools teach moral values more effectively than state schools?

Dear Penelope

I have a feeling you are waiting for me to say yes and then you will pounce. I spent much of my childhood reading public school stories in which good always triumphed over evil, but I know the reality too well to claim that, when it comes to teaching moral values, independent schools are superior to state schools. They are not inferior either. On this issue schools do not divide on fee-paying and non-fee-paying lines.

All schools teach moral values whether they set out to do so or not. A school is a moral community where, by design or by default, moral lessons are taught. Just as they do at home, the pupils draw conclusions from the way the authorities react when things go right and things go wrong. It is impossible for teachers to shirk this part of their role. They may be reluctant to come down on one side or another, or to say what behaviour is right or wrong because they do not wish to be 'too judgemental', but their neutrality still points to a moral. If the teachers refuse to commit themselves why should the children bother?

If all schools teach moral lessons whether they intend to or not, how do we know whether some schools do so more effectively than others?

I would not begin by looking at the curriculum. Attempts have been made to put moral teaching on the curriculum, but

I think they are misguided. It implies that the teaching of moral values can be taken care of by a specialist in classes allotted to the subject. Yet every aspect of the school's life is part of the moral syllabus and every member of staff is a teacher of moral values.

I think we should start by identifying the moral values themselves to gauge how well they are reflected in the school's priorities. Is the school seen to prefer honesty to dishonesty, self-control to self-indulgence, consideration for others to rudeness or deliberate cruelty, open-mindedness to bigotry, moral courage to moral cowardice? It is not easy to *measure* the school's performance in any of these areas, so a moral league table is, happily, not on the cards. But there is evidence, if you look for it, of whether the teaching of moral values is woven into the fabric of the school, or whether it is just something the head remembers from time to time when he is taking morning assembly.

The memory of morning assemblies makes me pause. Did anything I said about moral values on those occasions have any effect at all on the way the pupils behaved? I think it did, but heads need to remember that however strongly they believe in what they are saying, some pupils will be unmoved and others will be day dreaming.

The words of a headmaster's homily may not be listened to carefully by the pupils, but they are not wasted. His action is a public reminder to the school that some behaviour is morally wrong, whether or not it breaks the school rules (and in the majority of schools neither stealing nor bullying are explicitly forbidden). But a head who rants on about moral values will soon appear ridiculous. The moral shot across the bows only works if it is used sparingly.

The head is bound to play a key role in the school's teaching of moral values. He sets the moral priorities to a much greater degree than the academic ones. Even the most powerful head has only limited influence on which subjects are taught, but can profoundly influence the school's moral position by the way he reacts and encourages his staff to react to the behaviour of the pupils.

I would look first for evidence of effective moral teaching in what the school authorities are seen to reward or punish and in what they insist on or choose to ignore. And I would search for signs of the simple, everyday moral lessons, not just the high-profile ones.

Bullying is a high-profile issue. Most schools do now take an unequivocal stand against bullying and most have a published anti-bullying policy. Such a policy presents a clear preference for the consideration of others and a refusal to ignore deliberate cruelty, but the success of moral teaching depends on the effectiveness of the policy. A written policy will not eliminate bullying unless it is seen to be implemented. The pupils learn a very different moral lesson if they believe that the primary purpose of the policy is to improve the school's image and reassure prospective parents.

Stealing is not such a high-profile issue, yet it is as common as bullying. Do the head and the staff take an equally unequivocal stand against this form of dishonesty? Stealing is difficult to prevent and the pupils know this, but effective moral teaching requires the school, at the very least, not to equivocate. Stealing is wrong. Its seriousness should not be diminished by euphemisms such as 'pilfering'. A person who steals is a 'thief'. 'You bloody thief,' A. S. Neill, head of Summerhill in the 1930s, called a girl who had been stealing. What a refreshing change from the polite evasions of today's more conventional headmasters. Nor should schools shift any part of the blame on to the victim who 'should not have left money lying around', or on to the 'rampant materialism of society'. Although the school authorities may find it difficult to catch a thief, what matters in moral teaching is not the clear-up rate but the way in which the authorities are seen to respond.

The simple, everyday occurrences which do not involve rewards or punishments provide perhaps the most effective teaching of moral values. A boy is dropped from the first

football team and does not want to give up his Saturday afternoon to play for the seconds in an away match. But the master
in charge insists, pointing out to the boy that he has a duty
to the school and to the other members of the team to play.
In such routine clashes of interests lie profound moral lessons.
We cannot suit ourselves when we have obligations to fulfil.

Duty and obligation are not concepts that schools are
comfortable with these days. I searched in vain through the
prospectuses of state and independent schools until I came
across this passage written by the headmaster in the latest
prospectus of Radley College in Oxfordshire and originally
used to address the school at his first assembly in 1991:

> I hope that Radley will offer you this wholeness in which
> your individuality prospers but always to the benefit of the
> community. Firstly, that will almost certainly mean that true
> self-discovery will be found in a sense of duty rather than in
> self-indulgence. Secondly, wholeness means the acceptance of
> responsibility rather than the seeking of privileges. Do not
> bother to come and see me about privileges. You have them
> in profusion. But if you want to take on responsibility, knock
> on my door.

If he believes what he writes, there is a good chance that
the teaching of moral values is effective at Radley College. But
other heads and other schools prefer to teach moral values
through subjects that are less demanding and, in their eyes,
more relevant than a sense of duty. Sponsored swims for
charity and practical projects to harness the pupils' enthusiasm
for protecting the environment are worthwhile in themselves,
but I do not think they are evidence that a school is teaching
moral values effectively. A young person's passion to save the
whale or the world should not be met by adult cynicism, but
neither should it be allowed as a substitute for applying fundamental moral values closer to home.

It is easier to be in favour of a better world than to be

considerate to the people you have to rub shoulders with every day. So, the boy who has to recognize his obligation to turn out to play for the second team learns a harder moral lesson than the pupil who swims for charity or collects paper for recycling. However petty the original incident may seem to the outside world, it is teaching him to put duty before self-indulgence. He may be resentful at the time, but teaching moral values is not about enabling pupils to experience the feel-good factor.

School authorities seem reluctant to draw moral lessons from everyday life – witness the almost audible sigh of relief with which those who have to take morning assembly greet a disaster. But heads and chaplains who dwell upon the shocks and horrors of the world are not achieving the moral impact they imagine. Nor are teachers who introduce subjects beyond their pupils' understanding. I remember a young teacher telling me that he had had 'a fascinating discussion about abortion' with a class of thirteen year olds. Fascinating for him perhaps, but a waste of time for them at their age.

But what of those difficult decisions about sexual relations and the use of illegal drugs with which young people are familiar – surely these are a more effective vehicle for moral teaching than whether a boy turns up for a match on a Saturday afternoon?

These decisions do raise moral questions, not just health questions as some teachers would like to believe, and they can be effective vehicles for moral guidance, but just because they are over-hyped, 'relevant' issues it may be difficult to disentangle the moral element in the debate. So I am inclined to believe that the more mundane and less-fashionable issues provide better opportunities for moral teaching. The underlying message is after all the same – in our behaviour we should always consider the effect on other people and treat them as we would wish to be treated ourselves.

But we need to keep the school's influence in perspective. For good or ill, the home is a far more powerful teacher of moral values, not least because the distillation of standards always arises from the immediate and the everyday. Experienced heads and teachers know that the most effective moral lessons also have to run the gauntlet of the pupils own code of behaviour, the morality of survival. But these limitations on the school's influence are no excuse for not trying to help pupils find firm ground in the moral relativism of society.

In this interpretation of what it means to teach moral values, I do not believe the independent schools are more effective than the state schools. I can see why parents might think they are. Many independent schools are Christian foundations. They are predominantly middle class. Some of the best known are boarding schools. If a middle-class boarding school with a chapel and a chaplain cannot teach moral values, who can?

However, honesty, self-control, consideration for others, open-mindedness and moral courage are not the property of the independent school, or the middle class. So we return, as so often in debates about education, to the difference between good schools and bad schools, not to the difference between state and independent.

It must be one of the defining characteristics of a good school that the head and the staff are tuned in to the moral issues which arise each day and know when and how to draw attention to them. The master in charge of the second team knew he had to insist that the boy played football on that Saturday afternoon. In a bad school, the master would have shrugged his shoulders and asked another boy to fill the place. There are teachers like that, who cannot be bothered to insist because they do not want the hassle or to 'spoil their relationship' with the boy, just as there are teachers who are too afraid of the pupils ever to pass moral judgement.

It is not easy to discover whether a school has at least a majority of teachers who will insist on the difference between right and wrong behaviour. Academic excellence is not much of a guide; in my experience brilliant teachers can be moral cowards. Nor can you rely on that middle-class boarding school with a chapel and a chaplain.

Some of these schools have remained true to their Christian foundation and are not afraid to insist on morals and manners, but others seem to cultivate a sort of affluent yobbishness in which consideration for others plays little or no part. If parents believe their children are less likely to learn bad language and bad manners in an independent school they are in for a shock, unless they choose carefully. One thing most independent schools do teach their pupils is how to put on a good act. However yobbish and foul-mouthed they may be when you are not around, they can be charming and courteous when it suits them. But I don't think you should be too critical of that. Social hypocrisy is not a bad thing to learn and it does not prevent the individual pupil from developing an awareness of moral values.

When you do come to consider schools for Bronwyn and want to assess whether the school takes the teaching of moral values seriously, you cannot do better than put the question directly to the head: 'Do you take the teaching of moral values seriously?' And when the head assures you that it is indeed one of the school's priorities, you can ask a second question: 'What exactly does that mean in practice?'

Yours sincerely
John Rae

24 Do independent schools still take religion seriously?

Dear Mr and Mrs Dryden

Most independent schools would say that they still take religion seriously, but I would make a distinction between the majority of independent schools where religion, like small classes, is one of the educational benefits on offer, and the minority where religious faith and educational practice are indivisible. Broadly speaking, the distinction is between Protestant schools and Roman Catholic ones, particularly those run by a religious order such as the Jesuits and the Benedictines.

That may seem too sweeping a generalization and one that is unfair to Protestant schools. I would justify it in this way. In the Protestant schools, the Christian ethos is manifest in Christian values rather than in Christian faith. As the head of a Protestant school puts it, 'The Christian ethos of the school is evident in many ways but it is clearly seen in the emphasis placed on charitable work and the commitment to community service activities'. In a Roman Catholic independent school, Christian values are also important, but they are not a substitute for faith. 'At the heart of our foundation lies the faith which is essential to the character of the school,' says the head of the oldest Catholic girls school. The head of a Benedictine boys school spells it out even more clearly: 'Fundamentally it is the Catholic faith that makes a Catholic school distinct: specifically Catholic moral values flow from that faith and are not a substitute for it'.

In a reversal of the Reformation, it is faith rather than works that distinguish a Roman Catholic school and good works rather than faith that distinguish a Protestant one. The trouble with the Protestant schools' approach is that in a secular age religion in the form of charitable work and community service easily becomes marginalized because it is not rooted in a faith which staff, pupils and parents all share. That is the reason why I question whether there are many Protestant schools that can still be said to take religion seriously.

However, I am not arguing that Catholic schools are superior to Protestant ones. In academic terms, there is a noticeable lack of Catholic schools near the top of the A level league table. Nor am I arguing that their approach to religion is better, only that they take religion more seriously.

If you send your children to a good Roman Catholic independent school they will be taught about the faith. 'The pupils need to be put in a position in which they can discover and understand their faith,' writes Dom Anthony Sutch, the head of Downside. 'That faith includes a teaching of the mysteries and precepts of the Church. So the Trinity, the Resurrection, the Immaculate Conception and other tenets are to be faced up to and explained and not abandoned in favour of easily digestible topics such as prejudice and discrimination.'

That is unequivocal. I do not think the head of a Protestant independent school would speak of teaching about the faith in those terms. While Protestant schools make the faith available, they appear also to adopt a position of neutrality. One of the best Anglican schools, King's School, Canterbury, which uses the cathedral as its chapel and has an ordained priest as its head, goes out of its way to emphasize its neutral stance: 'The school is an Anglican establishment ... but pupils of other religions are freely admitted. The pattern of worship is flexible and the object is to arouse awareness rather than indoctrinate. Religious Studies is taught throughout the school. Those who wish it are prepared for confirmation.'

King's School's almost throwaway line about confirmation is typical of what in many Protestant schools seems to be a take-it-or-leave-it attitude to religion. The contrast with the Catholic schools is striking. When the great Benedictine foundation at Ampleforth, North Yorkshire, offers to Catholic boys 'a full religious education in the Roman Catholic faith' and 'a thorough grounding in the fullness of the Catholic tradition', it is not referring to an optional extra.

Does taking religion seriously imply indoctrination? For Catholic boys and girls in Catholic schools there must be an element of indoctrination that goes beyond disinterested teaching, but from my knowledge of these schools it certainly does not go as far as proselytizing, let alone brainwashing. The Benedictines and Jesuits know that a faith not freely chosen is unlikely to last.

If I were a Roman Catholic, I would not hesitate to send my children to one of the leading Catholic independent schools, but in recent years some Catholic families have had doubts about the wisdom of that course. League tables have exposed the relatively poor academic results of Catholic schools and that has put a strain on Catholic loyalties; a situation which has not been helped by the fact that some leading Protestant schools have made a discreet pitch for the Catholic market – Eton, for example, appointed an urbane and sophisticated Jesuit to minister to Catholic pupils.

In response to this trend, the leading Benedictine schools in particular have had the sense not to water down their Catholicity but to restate their belief in the value of a Catholic education in a Catholic school. Whatever arrangements a Protestant school makes for its Catholic pupils, they argue, it can never provide 'a thorough grounding in the fullness of the Catholic tradition'.

The monks are shrewder strategists than the heads of some other boarding schools short of pupils. Distinctiveness offers one of the best hopes of survival in a shrinking market; and though the monks would deplore the jargon, there will always be a niche market for schools which really do take their religion seriously.

I find it harder to generalize about Anglican independent schools because they include some, such as the Woodard Schools, that are self-consciously Anglican in their foundation and their ethos and others where the Church of England has a mention in the prospectus but no presence in the life of the school. The common denominator appears to be that while Christian values and Anglican ritual have their place, facing up to the fundamental tenets of the faith is not on an Anglican school's agenda.

The same inhibition about teaching pupils to understand the faith characterizes other Protestant independent schools. Some Methodist schools have all but abandoned Methodism. The only hint of conviction I found was the refusal of Methodist governors to approve an application for funds to the National Lottery because the Methodist church had always opposed gambling. One head told me bluntly that to emphasize the Methodist connection would be bad for recruiting. Schools founded by the Congregational church have similarly lost contact with their origins, though the two that I know well, Bishop's Stortford College, in Hertfordshire, and Taunton School, in Somerset, have retained the unpretentious flavour their founders preferred. The eight Quaker independent schools try to preserve a distinctive ethos, but as the majority of pupils are non-Quakers, following the Quaker tradition is more a matter of style than content.

With Roman Catholic independent schools parents know what sort of religious commitment they are buying, but with the Protestant independent schools they will be less clear of the situation. Most Protestant schools still require pupils to attend some religious services, though less and less frequently. Few members of the teaching staff attend apart from housemasters and housemistresses who are on duty. In most schools the head is required to be a Christian (though no longer 'a communicant' or 'practising'). Few heads would wish to be cross-questioned on the tenets of their faith. The implicit theme of their homilies to the pupils is deeds not faith; it matters less what you believe than how you treat other people. Those who wish to be confirmed are duly prepared for this religious step, but the number who wish to be confirmed is dwindling each year.

This distancing of the schools from their Christian foundations has been going on for a long time, though the arrival of non-Christian pupils to fill empty beds has made it easier to justify. Tolerance of other religions is now much in vogue. Schools reflect the secular mood of contemporary society, but in a longer perspective they also reflect the English approach to religion. What people believe is their business. Religious enthusiasm should be discouraged – especially among the young – and you will not find hand-clapping and speaking with tongues in school chapels. Pupils should experience religion, but not too intensely, and think about its implications, but not too deeply.

It is possible to argue that the Protestant schools never took religion seriously and that today's approach is less hypocritical than the church parades and automatic confirmations of the past. Whether today's approach will satisfy your requirements as a parent I cannot judge, but I suggest that when you visit a school you ask to see the school chaplain. Very few prospective parents ask this, yet the chaplain is more likely to give you an accurate account of the school's approach to religion than the head, who may be tailoring his answers to what he perceives to be the customer's expectations.

If the approach to religion is a key factor in your choice of school, it is worth considering whether that approach influences any other factors which contribute to the school's performance. Is there a correlation between taking religion seriously and poor academic performance? Are morals and manners better in schools that take religion seriously?

Ampleforth and St Mary's, Ascot, are the only Roman Catholic schools likely to appear in the top one hundred of the A level league table. In general, the academic performance of Catholic independent schools is mediocre or poor. The same is true of the Woodard Schools, Anglican schools that explicitly claim to take their religion seriously. On the other hand there are Anglican schools which take religion seriously – such as St Mary's, Calne, a girls' boarding school in Wiltshire – that produce consistently good academic results. If there is a correlation between taking religion seriously and academic performance, in the case of the Catholic schools it is because they are appealing to a niche market and cannot afford to be too selective. The Woodard Schools, too, cannot afford to be too selective; most are small boarding schools in a declining market. So I doubt whether taking religion seriously in itself affects academic performance one way or the other.

You might expect there to be a correlation between the extent to which the school takes religion seriously and the behaviour of the pupils, but I know of no evidence that this is the case. A taxi driver told me that although he was not a Catholic he sent his children to a local Catholic school because 'Catholic schools are strict'. It is a widely-held belief that discipline is better in Catholic schools. That may be true in the state sector, but it is not true of the independent sector. Discipline in Catholic independent schools is neither better nor worse. You should not expect a school's religious commitment to provide added protection for your child against bullying or illegal drugs. What may be true, however, is that moral values learnt in a Roman Catholic school are more likely to survive into adult life because they are rooted in faith and not just in classroom discussion. In this respect, choosing a school that takes religion seriously may prove a good, long-term investment, but you should not expect a quick return.

Yours sincerely
John Rae

25 Do schools still take sport seriously?

Dear Mr and Mrs Fry

Most independent schools take sport seriously, but that does not mean what it used to when compulsory games were the school's way of encouraging conformity and allegiance. Most state schools would like to offer a comprehensive sports programme, but few are in a position to do so. One of the most striking contrasts between independent and state schools is in the provision of sporting facilities. A leading independent school with twelve hundred pupils has twenty match squares for cricket; the London Oratory, a comprehensive school with the same number of pupils, has access to one cricket square which is some distance from the school and belongs to the local authority.

While state schools struggle to provide opportunities for sport, independent schools are adopting an increasingly professional approach to the achievement of sporting excellence. It is not just a question of spending millions on up-to-date facilities. Professional coaching is now generally available in a wide range of sports for the individual as well as for the team; and sports scholarships, once banned in independent schools, are now openly given.

A profound change has occurred in the independent schools' attitude to sport. Sporting achievement has become an end in itself, not a means to an end as it was for a century or more when the spirit of 'athleticism' ruled in public schools. Athleticism, the worship of games and of those who were good at them, flourished between the 1860s and the 1960s. It began as a way of diverting the schoolboy mob from more anarchic pursuits and developed into a religion with its own rituals and symbols, its own gods and moral code. Because games were thought to develop a manly character and character was more valued than intellect, they took precedence over academic work not only in the minds of the pupils but in the minds of the adults as well. 'Of course you needn't work, Fitzmilksoppe,' says the headmaster in a Punch cartoon of 1889, 'but play you must and shall.'

Athleticism proved remarkably tenacious despite its critics. Only in the late 1960s, when the pupils rejected conformity, did the edifice of compulsory team games begin to crack. What finished athleticism off was the realization that academic work would have to take precedence if the schools were to continue to attract customers. Fitzmilksoppe's A level results are now important to the school's future as well as to his own. He need not play cricket, but work he must and shall.

I never cease to admire the skill with which Britain's independent schools adapt to changing realities; it is the perfect riposte to those who think that headmasters and headmistresses do not understand how market forces work. The successful transformation of athleticism, which was hostile to academic achievement, into the new sporting ethos, which complements the schools' pursuit of academic excellence, is remarkable.

You will discover that the heads of independent schools are at pains to point out that the new professionalism does not signify that the old ideals of sportsmanship are forgotten. On the contrary, the independent schools see their role as helping to ensure that the spirit of the game remains untarnished, however professional the coaching may be. It is an attitude that I find both appealing and a little arrogant. There are other, less privileged people who value sportsmanship just as much; and when one independent school is paying over £100,000 a year in discounted fees to ensure a supply of good rugby players, a high moral tone is unwise.

One of the characteristics of the new ethos is the realization that individuals, not just school teams, should be encouraged to achieve sporting excellence. Athleticism had its heroes, but it was their contribution to the team that made them so. Sports such as tennis, track-and-field athletics and swimming, were less admired and in some schools actively discouraged because they were thought to foster individuality. That attitude is now obsolete. There is a much wider choice of sports available and both the pupils and the adults are just as proud of the boy or girl who competes well as an individual, in regional or national championships, as they are of the team that is victorious against traditional rivals.

This willingness to accommodate individual preference in sport and to accord all sporting excellence equal esteem owes something to the admission of girls to boys' independent schools and to the development of co-education. Though some girls' boarding schools had imitated aspects of athleticism, they were never so obsessed with team games and in general took a more mature approach to sport.

If any individual can be said to have led the way in this fundamental change in the independent schools attitude to sport it is Jack Meyer, who founded Millfield School, in Somerset, in 1935. Meyer was one of the most influential, but least well-known, innovators in independent education. He strongly believed in finding out what individual boys and girls were most likely to be good at and then providing them with the opportunity to develop their potential. That entailed sustaining as wide a range of academic and sporting choices as possible. If he had an educational philosophy it was that developing an individual's talent in one direction helped to build the confidence to succeed in other areas. The dyslexic pupil who trained hard to become an Olympic swimmer gained the self-confidence to cope with dyslexia as well.

Heads of conventional independent schools were suspicious of Meyer's approach. Allowing individual choice seemed subversive to schools still wedded to conformity and athleticism.

They accused Meyer of acting more like a talent scout than a headmaster and of offering cut-rate fees to the parents of talented athletes, something they would be doing themselves by the 1990s. They refused to play matches against Millfield and barred Meyer from attending their exclusive Headmasters' Conference.

Meyer was an entrepreneur and ahead of his time; the school he founded is now more mainstream, but Millfield has retained its emphasis on developing the talents – and not just the sporting promise – of the individual.

Millfield is the best example of the new approach to sport in independent schools. The range of sports available is astonishing; the senior pupils may choose from forty different sports and, if they wish, pursue them to the highest level. Beginners and established talents in their field have access to expert coaching and the school's organization is flexible enough to allow individuals to compete in whatever regional or national championships are appropriate. There are none of those childish arguments about 'major' sports and 'minor' sports that occurred so frequently under the old dispensation.

The facilities reflect the school's philosophy. The only full-size Olympic swimming pool in a British school is found at Millfield.

In most independent schools the individual now gets a much more professional deal in terms of opportunity, coaching and facilities. Nor have the team games suffered as the high priests of athleticism argued they would. Schools now put out a greater number of teams per age group than ever before, so that boys and girls at different levels of skill have a chance to play in matches. The number of pupils involved in team sports is impressive. A 1994 survey of 157 independent boys schools found that 37,000 – an average of 150 a school – were committed to cricket, not because they were compelled to be, but because they wanted to be. The standard of coaching for teams has improved too. The enthusiastic amateur who took the junior colts for rugby, as well as teaching history, and urged on his team from the touchline by blowing a hunting horn, now has a coaching qualification.

Do independent schools still take sport seriously? They take it more seriously in that they treat each sport and the individual's desire to excel in it with respect. They do not, however, see sport as a means to an end, or assume that a boy or girl who is good at sport is a natural leader. Nor do they give sport precedence over academic work. It is a change for the better.

Hero-worshipping talented games players is part and parcel of growing up. In the earlier days of athleticism it was often blown wildly out of perspective, not least because it was encouraged by over-grown adolescents on the staff. In today's schools, sporting excellence is admired for what it is, similar to achievement in other fields, such as drama or music. To say that the captain of rugby has no more prestige than Fitzmilk-soppe would be stretching a point, but the extreme bias in favour of physical rather than intellectual values is a thing of the past.

There may be any number of reasons why some schools excel at particular sports: tradition, geography, a gifted and single-minded coach; and, in a few cases, deliberate policy to use distinction in one sport as a marketing tool. I think you should be exceedingly wary of this ploy. A genuine centre of excellence that adds value to the life of the school is very different from an attempt to fill empty beds and to distract attention from the school's poor academic record. There are examples of both types in the independent sector. A boarding school with falling numbers and a low position in the academic league tables may decide that a reputation for excellence in soccer or horse-riding will attract the attention of a shrinking market. The facilities and opportunities to enjoy and excel at those sports may be superb, but the rest of what the school has to offer is probably not worth the money you will have to pay.

An example of a genuine centre of excellence, which adds

value to a good school, is the tennis centre at Queenswood, a girls boarding school in Hertfordshire. Queenswood is not a one-sport school, or a recent convert to sporting excellence, but it has developed its interest in tennis to a point where it stands out from all other schools. High-powered coaching and the biggest clay-court complex in the country naturally attract gifted young players. Girls who are of county standard and above are offered a special programme which combines academic work and tennis to give them a realistic chance of success in both. But the treatment of the elite does not discourage the others; instead, it raises their expectations. For the future tennis stars there are obvious advantages in being educated in a school where other things matter too.

Other schools that excel at particular sports include Eton, which dominates school rowing and Tonbridge, in Kent, which is the most consistently successful cricketing school. In soccer, the independent schools run their own knock-out competition, which has been won in the last three years by day schools in the northwest: King's School, Chester, St Bede's, Manchester, and Queen Elizabeth's Grammar School, Blackburn. In rugby, one of the few sports in which state schools have a chance to compete on equal terms with independent schools, there is no clear winner, but the most consistently successful are probably Colston's Collegiate School in Bristol, Millfield and Ampleforth, all independent schools. It is interesting that where a state school with a strong rugby tradition exists, such as the Royal Grammar School at Lancaster, it has little difficulty defeating most of the independent schools in the area.

Rugby is a realistic option for state schools that want to take sport seriously because it is cheap. The same is true of cross-country running, another sport at which state schools may succeed. But few state schools have the resources to excel at cricket and if they do have tennis courts it is, as one head put it to me, with 'a superior car park surface'.

It is no surprise therefore that the state schools which are successful at sport are also those that shine academically. The

Royal Grammar Schools at Lancaster and High Wycombe and the Judd School in Tonbridge represent the best of that tradition combining hard work and hard play, which few of the old public schools could match. Even today, the ability of these state schools to produce good A level results *and* good sports teams puts some of the independent schools, with more generous staffing and superior facilities, to shame.

But these state schools are the exception. Most state schools do not take sport seriously. Most independent schools do. If you want your son and daughter to go to a school where they will have the opportunity to discover which sport they have an aptitude for, and to develop their talent to a high level, you will have to pay fees unless you live near one of the exceptional state schools.

Yours sincerely
John Rae

26 Whatever happened to character and leadership?

Dear Margaret

Whether we like it or not, the pursuit of individual success – which for most pupils means good A level results – is probably uppermost in the minds of parents when they send their children to an independent school. They want their children to get on in life and if good A levels are what it takes, that is what they will pay for. Every survey of why parents pay fees puts high academic standards at the top. That would not have been the case for previous generations, but it is true today. But while academic standards top the poll, for many parents 'character training' is not far behind. So you cannot be the only parents who wonder how far these other elements in a traditional education have been marginalized by the increased emphasis on academic success.

In the old public schools the concepts of character, leadership and service were closely linked. Learning to conform as a junior trained your character, which eventually qualified you for leadership as a prefect, where you enjoyed status and privilege in return for serving the community. For over a hundred years this simple, but effective, formula produced thousands of loyal public servants, notably for the civil and military control of the Empire.

The withdrawal from an imperial role in the 1950s, the revolt against authority and conformity in the late 1960s and early 1970s, and the increasing awareness of the importance of academic success in the late 1980s and early 1990s, left the heads of independent schools, and of those state schools that still felt an affinity with them, uncertain of what sort of character, leadership and service they should be trying to promote and nurture.

The issue of leadership clearly illustrates the heads' dilemma. Some heads are so unsure of what qualities are needed, and of how to develop them, that they hire a commercial firm to run courses on leadership for potential prefects. The courses use the language of industry rather than public service; senior pupils are helped 'to make the transition from the shop floor to managerial positions'.

You may think things have come to a pretty pass when heads have to pay outside experts to train their prefects, but the practice reflects the changing interpretation of what leadership is about and of what role senior pupils should play in running the school. The need for change had its origins in the revolt against authority. Sometime in the late 1960s and early 1970s, the school prefect threw his hand in. It happened at different times in different schools, but the reason was always the same: senior boys and girls wanted to identify with their peers, not lord it over them. In some schools, the prefects disappeared altogether, but in most they remained, shorn of the real power they had once possessed and uncertain of what they were supposed to do. When younger pupils started calling prefects by their Christian names it was clear a new style of leadership was required.

If you visit schools today and talk with senior boys and girls in positions of responsibility – prefects, monitors, colour bearers – you will quickly realize that the new style of leadership is still evolving. If they retain the power to punish it is only with irksome tasks. They have had to learn the skill of persuading people to do things they do not want to do, without resorting to threats. Some try shouting, but most try reason. They still perform a number of traditional tasks, such as supervising meals, policing the tuck-shop queue and putting the juniors to bed. They are, as they always have been, ambivalent towards reporting crime – prepared to shop the thief or the bully, reluctant to report an illicit drinker or occasional cannabis user. This distinction, which is widely approved of in the pupils' underworld if not in the head's study, is between those who do harm to others and those who may be harming themselves. I have sat in on a number of regular meetings – typical of those which take place with the head and the prefects of a school – and have been struck by how often the head has to remind the prefects that it *is* their job to enforce the school rules and by how often the prefects want to negotiate some trivial concession, not for themselves but for all the senior pupils. It is not from shop floor to management that they are making the transition, it is from shop floor to shop steward.

Heads argue that the new style of prefect has to have skills that are useful in modern society, more managerial than authoritarian, but I doubt whether that will satisfy the first-time buyers of independent education who thought that learning how to take orders as a preparation for giving them was what independent schools were all about. As one father put it, 'You either tell others what to do in life, or for ever more get told what to do.'

Such sentiments jar with the heads of contemporary independent schools. Their present dilemma is that they need the senior pupils to help run the school, but neither they nor the senior pupils want that role to consist primarily of telling others what to do. The heads are keen to give boys and girls opportunities to exercise responsibility – not only as prefects, but also in the Combined Cadet Force and in games – but they themselves are not sure what type of leadership they are preparing their pupils for, or whether they should be consciously preparing them for leadership at all. In the United States, the heads of independent schools almost always mean 'business leaders' when they talk about preparing their pupils for leadership, but the heads in this country have not reached that point yet.

The heads of independent schools may be genuinely uncertain about leadership, but they appear to be hypocritical rather than uncertain when their attention is turned towards service. In their sermons and speech day addresses they imply that the spirit of service, especially the obligation to put something back into society if you have enjoyed advantages, is still part of the schools' ethos. But the heads know, as do their listeners, that the principal aim of those who have had a good education in late twentieth-century Britain is to make money. With few exceptions, independent school pupils do not intend to devote their lives to any form of public service, but rather to careers that command a high salary.

'The school devotes one afternoon a week to the idea of service to the community both within the school and at large', reads a typical prospectus entry, but community service at school does not automatically translate into service to the community in adult life. The sixth formers who visit old ladies and work with handicapped children may have a genuine desire to be of service, but the sixth form is usually where it ends.

Ambiguity about leadership and a limited commitment to the idea of service are closely linked. The reason for this should catch your eye when you study school prospectuses. The emphasis today is on the individual. Heads are keen for the prospective parent to know that the school caters for the individual and actively encourages individuality. Any school which made that promise fifty years ago would have been labelled 'progressive' and regarded as unsound, because character training was thought to depend on the curbing of individuality.

There has since been a decisive shift in the schools' attitude, not only away from a particular version of character training, but also from the belief that character can or should be trained to produce a desirable type of adult. Today's heads would vigorously reject any suggestion that they are producing a type. Instead they stress that they are producing individuals by giving pupils opportunities to develop self-knowledge, to discover through a variety of challenges their strengths and weaknesses, and to learn how to make the best of the character they have inherited.

In practice, though, I think heads are ambivalent towards the cult of the individual. Many heads dislike what they regard as the 'naked individualism' of society and try to temper it with the other two elements of leadership and service. One of the aims of Charterhouse School in Surrey, for example, is to 'promote a sense of individuality together with a sense of duty to friends and society'.

Whether any school succeeds in getting this balance right is doubtful. Schools are not monasteries and convents 'out of the swing of the sea'; thanks to the media, they are powerfully influenced by the fashion and mood of the times. Even in more cloistered days, there was a wide gap between the head's ideals and the pupils' response; for every boy at Rugby who took Dr Arnold's sermons seriously, there must have been many others who simply let it flow over them and got on with their lives. Today the head's ideals are more directly in competition with those of home and society as well. When I asked the head of the Oratory, a popular Roman Catholic state school, how he selected pupils, he replied that he chose those where the values of the home were in harmony with the values of the school. Other heads seldom have that luxury. Independent school parents are in favour of a sense of duty, but not if it gets in the way of their ambitions for their children. They pay lip service to sportsmanship and fair play, but when you hear them on the touchline you realize that winning is what really matters. Heads of independent preparatory schools, in particular, are regularly appalled by the aggressive behaviour of some parents at school matches.

You may find my comments too pessimistic. They are not intended to be. The gap between the head's ideals and the pupils' lives has never been of much consequence. But in recent years a different and more dangerous gap has opened up between the values of home and the values which the head thinks the school should be promoting. This hits independent schools particularly hard because in the past they have been able to rely on a similar identity of interest between the parents' aspirations and the schools'.

It is this gap more than anything else that makes it difficult for heads to say where the school stands on your question about character. Don't be put off by the uncertainty. A head who produces a pat answer has not thought very deeply about your question. But if you hope that schools will return to the priorities and practices of previous generations, you will be disappointed. Even if heads wanted to turn the clock back, they could not do so. They have to find a way of making sense of character, leadership and service in the modern context. I think they will succeed with leadership, but I think they will fail to persuade their pupils to consider a life of public service any more. I do not know how the struggle between home and school will be resolved, but I expect that the pursuit of individual success, particularly success which brings material rewards, to be the dominant theme in independent schools for many years to come. While the head preaches about Mother Teresa, the pupils will dream of becoming Richard Branson.

Yours sincerely
John Rae

Part Four

ADAPTING YOUR STRATEGY TO SUIT YOUR CHILD'S REQUIREMENTS

27 If our children turn out to be gifted, should we send them to special schools?

Dear Robert and Susannah

There are many variations on the theme of giftedness. The use of the word 'gifted' itself leads us straightaway into controversy, because it implies a natural talent – an inherited gift – and some people find that idea too elitist; they would prefer to believe outstanding talent is randomly distributed. Others have too narrow a view of what it means to be gifted. They associate it only with precocious ability in mathematics and music. But giftedness comes in many different forms and develops at different speeds. An outstanding creative or literary talent may not show its hand at all in childhood. Men and women the world now thinks of as being unusually brilliant may have revealed nothing of their talents at school. The opposite may also be true. The precocious child may not be gifted after all, just shooting ahead like a child who grows fast only to be caught up by other children a few years later.

I assume you are wondering what to do if one of your children turns out to be unusually bright (less of a mouthful than 'unusually advanced intellectual ability'). One way of finding out how clever children are is by an intelligence test which produces an Intelligence Quotient or IQ score. Intelligence tests favour those who are familiar with the sort of learning being tested, so they are not the last word on your child's brain power, but they are a useful snapshot. Children whose chronological age and mental age are much the same will have an IQ of around 100. Children whose mental age is ahead of their chronological age will have an IQ that is higher. About 2 per cent have IQs above 130 and 1 per cent above 140. To put that into perspective, at highly-selective academic schools there are a few pupils with IQs above 140, a large number with IQs above 130 and few with IQs under 130. It is unlikely that there are many pupils with IQs under 120.

The pupils with the highest IQs do not always do better at A level than those with IQs ten or more points lower. This is not because the teachers failed to recognize their giftedness, but because these pupils often lack crucial qualities of character. A strong will, a driving ambition and a capacity for hard work are needed to turn high intelligence into academic or any other form of success. I have known very gifted pupils whose high intelligence has never been put to any use. All that early promise has led only to a routine job, membership of a society for people who need reassuring that they are in the top 1 per cent and the satisfaction of completing *The Times* crossword before the commuter train reaches Victoria. Cleverness is not enough.

And, just as high intelligence without the strength of character to harness it to some purpose seldom achieves anything significant in adult life, so less dazzling IQ scores linked to real determination will almost always make their mark.

You may think this strengthens the argument for sending unusually bright children to special schools, but I am convinced that there is no better environment for these children than a good all-round school with a selective entry and high academic standards. If they are taught at home, or in some exclusive hothouse advertised as a school for gifted children, their sense of specialness is reinforced in a way that may actually do more harm than good. Exceedingly bright children need to know that there are other youngsters who are just as bright in other ways and have other gifts which are just as valuable. They need to learn tolerance, too, of those who think less clearly and quickly than themselves. Above all, they need the things which neither home nor hothouse can provide: a wide choice of friends (and enemies), games to play and interests to pursue. Just because you have found the sum of the first hundred integers at the age of eight, does not mean that you can opt out of a fully-rounded education.

There are two problems you may face as a parent if one of your children does turn out to be unusually bright. You may not, for financial or geographical reasons, have access to an academic school. The National Association for Gifted Children believes that 'state primary and secondary schools can provide admirably for gifted children', but I doubt whether that is true of the majority of state schools. The state secondary schools which do have high academic standards, and the primary schools that feed them, *can* provide. But some state primary schools are very reluctant to make special provision, whether it is for very intelligent pupils or for pupils with learning difficulties, and some state school teachers are ideologically opposed to arrangements, such as grouping pupils by ability in different subjects, that would enable the brighter children to be stretched. Hostility towards pupils who are 'too clever by half', which was a characteristic of the old public schools, is now more likely to be found in the staff rooms of some state schools. In a Kafkaesque twist, some unusually bright children have actually been diagnosed as having learning difficulties. It is not deliberate of course, but I cannot help thinking of Soviet dissidents being put into mental hospitals.

If you have an unusually bright child in a school that is not sympathetic to his or her needs, you should seek the advice of the National Association for Gifted Children about the correct procedure to follow. But I fear you will find that the local education authority's bureaucracy moves very slowly and that, in the end, the attitude of the school will not have changed. Better perhaps to concentrate your energy providing stimulus for your child outside school (and here the NAGC can help), while you explore the possibility of moving close to a good primary school and of obtaining financial help from a suitable independent school. The heads of respected independent schools are in the talent business and may be more sympathetic to a direct approach from the parents of a very bright child than you might expect. But don't move your child out of the frying pan into the fire. You are looking for an academically-selective school that offers a genuinely all-round education not a 'swot-shop' where the meaning of life is measured in A level grades.

I gather it is your fifth child, Charles, you are both concerned about and that the older children are happily settled in state schools where you live in Shrewsbury. As three of those older children are girls, it is worth mentioning the evidence that unusually bright girls are less likely to fulfil their potential than boys and this is despite the fact that up to the age of sixteen girls appear to do better academically. The point is that some could do better still. That faultless, tidy work handed in on time – so unlike the boys' – may be as far as unusually bright girls are prepared to go in a mixed ability, co-educational school; for despite all the changes of recent years, society still encourages some girls to undervalue their talents. Are you sure Charles is the only potentially gifted child in the family?

I am in favour of sending mentally gifted children to good academic schools, not to special schools. I am not in favour of accelerating them so that they are being taught with children two or three years older than themselves; that used to be done with scholars in the old public schools, where the general level of ability was lower than it is now, but the practice has been abandoned. Academic schools do encourage bright pupils to take some examinations early, but there is a difference between GCSE mathematics at fourteen and A level examinations at the age of nine or ten which a few highly intelligent children have been encouraged to take by their parents. These children are not freaks to be exhibited in the travelling circus of the popular press.

It is sometimes argued that bright children will be so frustrated at being held back that their behaviour will deteriorate;

some parents of disruptive children console themselves with the thought that he or she is a gifted child unappreciated by the teacher. But, as yet, there is no reliable research evidence that associates unusually high intelligence with emotional problems, or that frustrated talent is bound to result in delinquent behaviour. A few very bright children are misdiagnosed and turn their talents elsewhere when the school fails to connect. The highly intelligent boy whose home and school cannot stimulate or satisfy may well end up as the leader of a street gang. Yet, contrary to popular belief, unusually bright children are not highly strung, eccentric loners or miniature versions of the absent-minded professor; they are exactly like other children except in their superior intelligence and they should be educated in good mainstream schools.

The mainstream school is not necessarily the right choice, however, for children who are gifted musically. There are good specialist music schools such as Chetham's School in Manchester, and Wells Cathedral School in Somerset, but there are also a few very strong music departments in mainstream independent schools. With musically gifted children you have a choice, which you do not have with unusually bright children, of various degrees of specialization in different types of school.

Chetham's and Wells Cathedral School are independent, but the fees of their musically gifted children are paid on a means-tested basis by the government under a scheme to encourage talent in music and dance. At Chetham's, 250 out of 300 pupils are being supported by the government's scheme, so that the school is in effect a national centre of musical excellence. Wells Cathedral School is a mainstream school that specializes in music. Of its 800 pupils many are talented musicians, but only 60 are supported by the government. Whereas Chetham's is uncompromisingly focused on music, the ethos at Wells favours musicians and music-making but within the framework of a normal school.

Government support for gifted musical children is politically uncontroversial. Subsidizing the education of unusually bright children provokes hostility, but giving musical children a head start presents no ideological dilemma; they are in a different race.

Whether a musically gifted child should go to an uncompromisingly specialist school, such as Chetham's or the much smaller Yehudi Menuhin School in Surrey, or to Wells Cathedral School, must to a large extent depend on whether the parents believe that music is going to be their child's life. The more certain parents are that this is going to be the case, the more I would be inclined to send the child to Chetham's.

There is another option and that is to send the child to one of the independent schools which do not specialize in music, but that have developed strong music departments. Almost all independent schools claim to have 'a thriving music department', but only a few attract sufficient numbers of talented pupils and teachers to interest the parents of a musically gifted child. These few, with characteristic single-mindedness, have decided to create an outstanding music department and have the money to offer generous scholarships and to recruit talented staff. The appeal of a good musical education in schools that have so much else to offer is beginning to draw some gifted musicians away from the specialist schools.

A rough-and-ready guide for parents would be this. If a child seems likely to become a performer of the first rank in a life dedicated to music, go to Chetham's or Yehudi Menuhin. If a child has undoubted talent, but it remains important to keep other academic and career options open, go to Wells Cathedral School. If the child's musical talent is always likely to take second place to a career in another field, go to a good independent school with a strong and varied music department. All these options are open to parents who cannot afford fees.

I cannot remember ever having read of a musical talent that did not show its hand until the teenage years. But nor can I think of a great writer, or religious or political leader, whose giftedness was there for all to see at the age of five. The late developers or the late bloomers as the Americans call them, are as intriguing as the precocious children. Is the late flowering programmed or does it require a trigger?

You say Charles never stops asking questions and has astonishing powers of concentration, particularly when he is putting his collection of shells and plants in order. All children who are four going-on five ask lots of questions, but the ability to concentrate on the job in hand is rare and may be a sign of high intelligence. Those whose gifts take a long time to blossom, however, may be dreamers who find it difficult to concentrate until they discover what it is they want to concentrate on.

Charles's collections and his methodological approach must owe something to your interest in natural history, Susannah. All those trays of butterflies cannot have escaped his notice. Don't ask me whether he has inherited your aptitudes or is just following your example. Attempts to quantify the influence of heredity and environment seem to me unreal. The genes are coded, but they are coded for potential, not destiny. Without the right environment an inherited talent is unlikely to develop its full potential, but the most stimulating environment cannot develop a talent that is not there.

If Charles continues to show signs of being unusually bright try to get him into an academically selective school, not a special school, but a good all-round school where there are other bright children and other gifts on display. I realize money is a problem and that you do not want Charles to be separated from his brother and sisters. But you have one of the top academic schools on your doorstep which gives scholarships to bright boys at the age of thirteen. Shrewsbury School is one of the best independent schools because it manages to combine good academic standards with excellence in other areas, such as sport. Why not go to see the headmaster, tell him about Charles and explain your financial position? If he is interested – and heads of good schools should always be interested in unusually bright children – you could also ask his advice about Charles's education until he is thirteen.

Give Charles all the encouragement you can and let me know from time to time how he is getting on. He may become the scientist you would have been if circumstances had been different, Susannah, but don't count on it. He has some of your genes, but he will be his own man.

Yours sincerely
John Rae

28 Are there independent schools that really do cater for the less able child and the dyslexic child?

Dear Mr and Mrs Munro

There is no connection between dyslexia and average or below average intelligence except that teachers may confuse one for the other. Nor is there any connection between dyslexia and high intelligence though some parents, citing Leonardo da Vinci, persist in believing that there is. The less able child and the dyslexic child both need what is now termed 'learning support', but the difficulties they experience in school are not the same, and should not be mistaken as such.

The independent sector claims that it can develop the potential of every child because it includes in its ranks not only high-powered academic schools but schools that specialize in helping children who are less able and children with specific learning difficulties, such as dyslexia. Assessing that claim is not easy because so many independent boarding schools have recently moved into the 'less able and dyslexic' market. There are now hundreds of independent schools that profess to give 'specialist help for dyslexics'.

From the schools' point of view, this is good marketing; they are offering a service to parents who fear that their less able or dyslexic children will lose out in state schools with large classes and limited funds. The problem for parents is to distinguish between the genuine article and the marketing ploy.

As far as the less able children are concerned, we need to be clear which children we mean. Most children going to independent boarding schools at thirteen qualify for entry by reaching a 'pass mark', expressed as a percentage, in the common entrance examination. If this exam was marked centrally we would have a better idea of whether independent schools were taking less able children, but each school marks the papers of its own candidates for entry: oversubscribed schools are tough, undersubscribed schools are generous. Or to put it another way, schools which are short of pupils fiddle the marks. They want candidates to pass, but they do not want to get the reputation for being a soft touch. They say they want to help less able children, but they do not want to be known as a school for less able children.

Although IQ scores have their limitations they are a much better guide to a child's academic ability than common entrance exams. In the context of independent schools, less able children fall into two categories. There are those who have an IQ of between 90 and 100, in other words they are of average, or slightly below average, intelligence, and who in the right school might be capable of obtaining one or two A levels. And then there are those with an IQ below 90, who are not going to take A level, but may alternatively choose to take vocational qualifications, such as a General National Vocational Qualification (GNVQ).

Parents with children in the second category invariably say they want their children educated in a good mainstream school, by which they usually mean a school that people have heard of. But comparatively few mainstream independent schools offer courses which lead to vocational qualifications. The best source of information on the schools that do offer these options is the Independent Schools Information Service.

It is easier to find the right independent school for children in the first category, but it is also easier to make a mistake. Almost all independent boarding schools that are not in the top flight academically will assure you that they can bring out the best in boys and girls, who in a more academic school would be thought to be incapable of taking A levels. I think your initial response should be scepticism. There is all the difference in the world between a school that has the experience and expertise for this task and a less proficient boarding school which is touting for business. Quite apart from whether the latter has the necessary expertise, it will have little else to offer your child. One of the essential qualities you should look for in a school for a less able child is that it is a good school in its own right.

There is only a small number of good schools that specialize in helping those with average, or slightly below average intelligence, to achieve more than might have been expected at A level. The market leader is probably Milton Abbey, a boys' boarding school in Dorset. Other schools, both single sex and co-ed, achieve similar results, but I suggest that in your search for the genuine article you use Milton Abbey as the touchstone.

While it is true that some very large schools, such as St Louise's Comprehensive College in Belfast, are famous for drawing out the potential of children of widely differing abilities, one of the characteristics of schools that specialize in helping this category of less able children is that they are small.

Milton Abbey has two hundred pupils. It offers a surprisingly wide choice of sporting and extra-curricular activities, so that a boy has to work hard not to be a star at something. 'Everybody here is reasonably famous,' I was assured by the boy who showed me round. To know and be known makes the pupils feel good about themselves and that helps to rebuild the confidence that took a knock when friends and brothers sailed into more competitive schools.

Although the competitive instinct has a free rein in sport, Milton Abbey is deliberately uncompetitive in the classroom. These boys are kindred spirits; no one calls anyone else 'thick'. Yet many believe that they have failed. Importantly, though, the school does not try to sweep that belief aside with easy platitudes. Instead it teaches failure in the sense that it encourages the boys to be realistic about what they can achieve with hard work. Gradually, very gradually in some cases, growing confidence and the feel-good factor push failure into the past.

Milton Abbey is not a perfect school. It still has the normal problems of an adolescent boarding school off the beaten track; and I have no reason to believe it is any better, or any worse, than other boarding schools at dealing with them. But it has had forty years in which to build experience and expertise in its specialist task. Boys whose academic ceiling was thought by their former headmaster to be a modest clutch of GCSEs are leaving school with two or three A levels. The grades vary and the most popular subject is business studies, not physics, but A levels they are and they open many more doors than the GCSEs would have done.

What is more, the self-confidence gained by the school's pupils is not the shallow 'effortless superiority' of the traditional public schoolboy, but the self-belief that comes from fighting back and proving the pessimists wrong.

Milton Abbey is the genuine article; its interest in these children is not a marketing ploy. If you want to know which the other genuine articles are, my advice is to keep three factors in mind. The school should be reasonably small, no more than three hundred pupils, but not so small that it cannot offer a wide range of non-academic activities; its interest in less able children should be well established and – most difficult to spot – there should be a touch of genuine idealism in what the school and its staff are trying to achieve. The best source of *factual information* is your regional office of the Independent Schools Information Service; the best source of *opinion* is the preparatory school heads in your area. One of the difficulties you will encounter is that there are very few independent day schools that really do cater for less able children. In many towns and cities, pressure on entry places has made these schools too selective academically to have either the know-how or the set-up required to help children of average intelligence. Good education for less able children in the independent sector is likely to entail boarding.

The need to distinguish between the genuine article and the

marketing ploy is even more important if your child is dyslexic, because in this case there are so many variables to be considered. The definition of dyslexia is still a controversial subject. One reason for this is that dyslexia is not a discrete condition, but a continuum: one dyslexic child's reading difficulty is not the same as another's; they occupy different places on the continuum. Another reason is that experts disagree about whether to include a condition such as 'number blindness' which many dyslexic children experience, or to give this a different name, 'dyscalculia', and regard it as a condition in its own right.

My view is that we should think of dyslexia as a continuum of learning difficulty, most commonly associated with reading, which children experience with varying degrees of severity, but always in their own way. It is thought that up to 10 per cent of children are dyslexic, that boys are more often and more acutely affected than girls and that dyslexia is probably hereditary. Because it is principally associated with reading difficulty, it is unlikely to be diagnosed before the age of five, though specially designed computer games may highlight the problem earlier.

Dyslexic children need special help. What sort and how much depends on the nature and severity of their particular difficulty. The problem for schools is that any expert help for individuals is expensive. Few state primary schools can cope, not because they are unwilling, though some prejudice against the 'middle-class word for laziness' persists, but because they cannot afford to. Some local education authorities provide help out of school; most do not. Parents who try to persuade their local authority to pay fees for an independent school which specializes in dyslexia face a long and often debilitating struggle. Parents have no right to such financial assistance unless a professional assessment of the child forms the legal basis of a 'statement of special educational needs', or in the jargon of local authority bureaucrats, unless the child is 'statemented'.

The practice is as Orwellian as the jargon. Every possible obstacle is put in the parents' path. I have even known a case where a school lied about a child's progress to undermine the parents' argument that he had special educational needs. In other cases, the authority involved has been known to claim dishonestly that all educational needs can be adequately met in its own schools.

It is against this negative background that provision for dyslexic children has proliferated in the independent sector. So many independent schools now say they cater for dyslexia that a new directory of them has been published by the Independent Schools Information Service. Catering for dyslexics can mean anything ranging from a specialist school for dyslexia, to a mainstream school where the staff have no special expertise but are said to be 'sympathetic'. I think you can rule out the latter; amateurs, however sympathetic, do more harm than good. Whether all the other schools – who profess their support for dyslexic pupils – are professional in their approach is doubtful. The market has expanded so fast it is impossible for anyone to monitor the quality of the service being offered.

The schools fall into three broad categories. The specialist schools that cater exclusively for dyslexic children are well-established, but if you are looking for an all-round education of which help for dyslexic pupils is a part, these are not the schools for you. They may, however, be the right school for a child whose dyslexia is so severe that other considerations are secondary.

The second and larger category is mainstream schools which have a dyslexia unit or learning support centre that is fully equipped and staffed by qualified personnel. From the point of view of the pupils and their parents, the advantage of this approach is that dyslexic pupils are able to participate in the normal life of a good school, with all its opportunities to develop excellence in other fields. The pupils with learning difficulties may be a majority in a small school, as they are at Stanbridge Earls School in Hampshire which is famous for its work with these children; or a small minority in a large school, as at George Watson's College in Edinburgh which is as famous for its academic and sporting results as it is for the success of its learning support centre and dyslexia unit. Both these schools are co-educational. At Stanbridge Earls, the children with learning difficulties are 80 per cent of a school with 190 pupils; at George Watson's, they are 10 per cent of a school with 2200 pupils.

These contrasting schools have in common a professional approach to pupils with dyslexia; they are the genuine article, not the marketing ploy. But I have also chosen them to illustrate how different the relationship between the dyslexia unit and the rest of the school can be, and how important it is for parents to visit the school to discover exactly how that relationship works.

At Stanbridge Earls, the character and priorities of the school reflect the needs of the pupils with learning difficulties. The maximum class size is ten children. Because boys are statistically more likely to have learning difficulties than girls, they are also more likely to be in the majority. The pace of the small school suits children of either sex who lack confidence in their own academic ability.

At George Watson's, helping children with learning difficulties is just one of many things the school does well. The balance of the sexes in the school reflects the balance in society. Boys and girls in the dyslexia unit receive one-to-one tuition, but their normal classes are the same size as in other independent day schools. One of the most interesting and appealing aspects of George Watson's is that the senior boys and girls who do not have learning difficulties provide support, by acting as scribes for example, for individual dyslexic pupils.

If one of your children does turn out to be dyslexic, I would advise you to start your search for the right school by looking at good mainstream schools with a dyslexia unit or learning support centre, that have a proven track record. Of course, much will depend on the nature and severity of a particular child's learning difficulty, and here you will need the guidance of a psychological assessment and of specific recommendations about the type of teaching and schooling required. If you need advice on how to obtain an assessment and recommendations, I suggest you consult either the Dyslexia Institute or the British Dyslexia Association.

In the majority of cases the recommendation will be that the child will benefit from being educated in a mainstream school which arranges for the child to be withdrawn from some ordinary classwork to receive specialist teaching. Although this *could* mean schools such as Stanbridge Earls and George Watson's, it *also* means schools where there is no dyslexia unit, but where specialist help is readily available.

These latter schools form the third and largest category. They are also the schools where the quality of the provision for dyslexic pupils is most difficult to assess. What counts is how well qualified the specialist help is, how thoughtfully the withdrawal from ordinary classwork is planned and how well informed about dyslexia the rest of the teaching staff are. If circumstances point you in the direction of one of these schools, pin down the head on these three issues. What qualifications does the specialist teacher have? What ordinary classwork is missed (French is an obvious choice)? What training has the rest of the staff had?

The law entitles children with special learning difficulties to have appropriate provision made for them. In reality lack of money and different priorities mean that few local education authorities meet that obligation. For the foreseeable future the only sure way to obtain a good education for a dyslexic child is in an independent school. The same is not necessarily true for a less able child, but some independent schools excel in turning pupils of average intelligence into credible A level candidates.

Yours sincerely
John Rae

29 What are the differences between the academic advantages of single-sex schools and the social advantages of co-education?

Dear Emily

Your letter makes me think you have been caught in the crossfire of the public relations battle between the head-mistresses of single-sex schools and the headmasters of those boys schools which have admitted girls; a battle that the head-mistresses are winning comfortably.

It all started in the seventies when an increasing number of boys' independent schools opened their sixth form to girls. Even the best girls' schools – Cheltenham Ladies College, Wycombe Abbey, St Paul's Girls' School – lost able pupils to the sixth forms of boys' schools, which in some cases were less successful academically. This was before the publication of comparative exam results, so parents were unaware just how much better their daughter's school was than the boys' school she was so anxious to join. Only when the A level league tables were published could parents see that schools such as Marlborough, the first to open its sixth form to girls, were well over a hundred places below the leading girls' schools.

For the headmistresses, the exodus of some of their best pupils was all the more difficult to bear when the headmasters could scarcely conceal their delight at finding a way of raising academic standards while increasing numbers. They accused the headmasters of being 'white slavers' who did not care for the welfare of the girls and they accused the girls who wanted to move of being only interested in the boys.

It was an ill-judged counterattack that proved ineffective. The headmasters must have thought they had won with ease. Mixed sixth forms proliferated and then in the eighties an increasing number of boys' independent schools decided to go fully co-educational, admitting girls at eleven or thirteen.

The headmistresses bided their time. Their strongest card was the excellent academic results of the leading, single-sex girls' schools. (The fact that other single-sex girls' schools produced some of the worst academic results in the independent sector would be overlooked.) If parents could be persuaded that the academic excellence reflected a universal truth that girls did better academically in single-sex schools, then the bandwagon of mixed sixth forms and co-education might be slowed down.

This more sophisticated strategy, devised by the Girls' Schools Association, was given a much-needed boost by the publication of academic league tables in the nineties. There was the evidence for all to see. Single-sex independent girls' schools dominated the top of the GCSE table *and* outperformed the co-educational schools at A level. In addition, the girls' schools' success was not limited to day schools. Single-sex boarding schools, such as Wycombe Abbey and St Swithun's, Winchester, did equally well at A level, reinforcing the belief that, for girls, single-sex education was superior.

Suddenly, the headmasters found themselves on the defensive. They decided to commission research which, they hoped, would prove that single-sex education was not, in itself, academically superior to co-education, notwithstanding the fact that the best single-sex girls' schools did very well.

The research confirmed that: 'Just because the single-sex schools do better, it does not follow that this is due to their single-sexness.' 'There is no evidence', the researchers concluded, 'that one type of schooling is more effective than the other in exam terms.'

Instead of publishing the research in a way that would assist their case, the headmasters released it to the press immediately prior to the publication of the 1995 academic league tables, in which the single-sex girls' schools would once again be the stars. It was a public relations gaffe that resulted in the research being ignored, or regarded as special pleading. Why should parents believe research when the league tables appeared to tell a different story?

The headmistresses had outmanoeuvred the headmasters by concentrating parents' minds on the academic results of the best single-sex schools. When academic qualifications count for so much, why risk your daughter's chances at A level for the sake of the supposed advantages of co-education? In many families, the decision you are finding difficult to make is no longer thought worth discussing. The only relevant question is which single-sex girls' school should their daughter apply for.

But the public-relations battle has confused two issues. The first is whether girls do better academically in single-sex schools. One can see why this might be the case. In mixed classes, particularly large ones, the boys may be more demanding of the teacher's attention and the teacher, taking the line of least resistance, may give the boys the attention they demand – therefore sidelining the girls' needs. It is possible, too, that in co-educational schools the cultural assumption that girls will be less good at mathematics and science still operates, though I would have thought that this prejudice must be working its way out of the culture by now. Above all, it is said that a single-sex school is more likely to develop a girl's self-belief – so that when she leaves school it is a career, whether medicine or management, that she is heading for and not the first job that comes along.

There is no doubting the academic success of girls from single-sex schools at A level and in university entry, but that is only true of girls from the relatively small number of *good* single-sex schools, not of girls from single-sex schools in general. Many single-sex girls' schools in the independent sector have poor academic records and it is unlikely that their pupils do better academically than they would have done in a co-educational school.

The second, related issue is whether single-sex schools, for boys or girls, are by their very nature likely to be more successful academically than co-educational schools. We all have this impression because so many of the strongest academic schools in this country are single-sex. But is this anything to do with their 'single-sexness', or is it just because their reputation for academic excellence attracts the most able pupils? The research commissioned by the headmasters concluded that it was the latter.

I agree with their findings, but in relation to both these issues I am prepared to believe that for girls the combination of selective entry and 'single-sexness' creates an especially strong motivation towards academic success. Or to put it another way, all pupils are likely to do well academically in selective schools, but girls may do even better if the selective school is single sex.

The trouble with co-education is that its benefits cannot be measured. In many countries they do not have to be; it is taken for granted that boys and girls should be educated together. But in this country until the late sixties co-education was the exception, particularly in those 'public schools' and grammar schools to which parents aspired to send their children. Even though comprehensive schools have now made co-education the norm in the state sector, the case for co-education still has to be argued, and many middle-class parents remain unconvinced of its merits.

I think some of the claims made for co-education are overstated. Is it really true that children educated in co-educational schools are more at ease with the opposite sex, have a richer and more rounded education and are better prepared to live in the 'real world', wherever that may be? And even if there is some truth in these claims, are they worth giving up a place in a good academic, single-sex school for? Perhaps they were in the days when pupils in single-sex schools, particularly boarding schools, were more cut off from the opposite sex than they are now. But today, if pupils at single-sex schools are at a disadvantage, either socially or in their emotional maturity, the disadvantage is short lived.

So, I wonder whether your dilemma is as acute as you suppose. If I were you, I would choose the school which seems to be best suited for Lucy academically and let the social side look after itself. That does not automatically mean single-sex. In the state sector, the best academic schools are single-sex; schools such as Chelmsford County High School for Girls, in Essex, and the Royal Grammar School, High Wycombe, in Buckinghamshire, for boys keep alive the single-sex grammar school tradition. In the independent sector, too, most of the successful academic schools are single-sex, the boys dominating the top of the A level league table and the girls the top of the GCSE league table.

But in the independent sector, if not the state, there are schools with mixed sixth forms and fully co-educational schools which are also successful academically. King's School, Canterbury, and Rugby, in Warwickshire, among boarding schools, and Portsmouth Grammar School and Hutchesons' Grammar School, in Glasgow, among day schools, are all fully co-educational *and* academically strong.

These schools are proof, if proof is needed, that high academic standards and co-education are not incompatible. The problem for parents, such as yourselves, is that the academic co-educational schools are few and far between. Of the top one hundred schools at A level, only about fifteen each year are co-educational and some of those only at the sixth-form stage. The way education has developed in this country means that parents who want high academic standards and co-education are rather limited for choice.

There is little chance of this situation changing. Although a greater number of boys' independent schools are becoming fully co-educational, they are not in the same class academically as King's Canterbury and Rugby. Some have opened their doors to girls purely because they are no longer viable as boys' schools. In that situation, the chances are that they offer neither true co-education, nor high academic standards.

Other things being equal, I would prefer to send my children to co-educational schools. But in Britain, other things are not always equal; and when Lucy is eighteen, good academic qualifications will be more important to her future than the less-marketable benefits of being educated with boys.

Yours sincerely
John Rae

30 What are the advantages and disadvantages of being at the same school from four to eighteen?

Dear Mr and Mrs Grenfell

That is an interesting question because the number of all-age schools that take pupils from four or younger to eighteen is increasing, though only in the independent sector. The strongest growth in numbers in this sector is for the ages two to six. There are no all-age schools in the state sector apart from those for children with special needs. The reasons for the increase are economic and competitive rather than educational, so you should not be led to think that the increase confirms the advantages of the all-age school.

All-age schools enjoy the economies of scale while keeping the different parts of the school relatively small. They may also have an edge in the competition for able pupils by recruiting so young.

The well-established, all-age schools are predominantly girls urban day schools, notably those in membership of the Girls' Public Day School Trust. Twenty-four of the twenty-five GPDST schools are all-age and a number of these have now opened nursery schools for the under-fours. As the trust also operates a Minerva Network – which offers support and information throughout a former pupil's working life from student days to retirement – these schools could almost be said to provide a cradle-to-grave service.

The academic strength of some GPDST schools, such as Oxford High School, Portsmouth High School and Sheffield

High School, helps to persuade parents that the advantages of the all-age school outweigh any disadvantages there may be in remaining at the same school for fourteen years.

For parents, the great advantage of an all-age school is that when their children are admitted at four, there are no more worries about which school to send them to and no more anxious waiting for the results of entrance exams. Some parents also believe that the continuity of an all-age school enables them to develop a satisfyingly close relationship with the school, so that they and their children become part of the school's family.

The family metaphor is a recurring one in discussions about all-age schools and has some authenticity if, for example, the teacher who taught your children the three Rs is there to share your pride when those children emerge as young adults at eighteen. So closely do some parents identify with the all-age school, that they experience an acute sense of loss when their children finally leave.

From the pupils' point of view, what appear to be the advantages – the teachers who know you, the friends who move up with you, the security of being accepted without further exams – may be disadvantages. What the headmistresses of all-age girls schools like to call 'a seamless education' may engender a false sense of security. For some children, being accepted for what they are at a young age may give them just the confidence they need to reveal later what they always might have been. But others need the stimulus of insecurity to bring out the best in them. Having the same pool from which to choose your friends for fourteen years may also have a negative effect, in this case on a child's ability to develop relationships.

As for teachers who know you well or think they do, they can be a drag. Just when you need someone to believe you are capable of reaching for the stars, there they are ready to dash your hopes with talk of realistic expectations. It cannot be a coincidence that in the early days of mixed sixth forms in boys' independent schools, so many applicants were girls from all-age schools. At the age of sixteen they had had enough. Was it really co-education they wanted, or a chance to start afresh with teachers who didn't know them?

The heads of all-age schools soon recognized the danger and gave their own sixth forms greater autonomy and a more distinctive character. Fewer girls now leave all-age schools at sixteen, but the desire for change after so many years at the same school will always be there. It was a factor the boys' schools considered before they moved into the all-age market, but they reckoned that unlike the girls' schools they were in no danger of losing pupils at the sixth form stage. Whether their confidence was justified remains to be seen.

In one respect the boys' all-age schools have made it more likely that they will lose some pupils along the way. The headmasters, unlike the headmistresses, have rejected the idea of a seamless education from four to eighteen. Almost all boys' all-age schools require pupils to take an internal exam at eleven, or Common Entrance at thirteen, to qualify for the senior school; and the all-age schools which recruit pupils to the senior school, at thirteen in particular, cannot afford to alienate the preparatory schools on whom they still depend for part of their thirteen-plus intake.

So in the boys' all-age schools one of the perceived advantages is missing. Acceptance at the age of four does not mean your child's education is secure for the next fourteen years. However, that may change as more independent schools jockey for position in the race to recruit the ablest pupils. The publication of academic league tables means that even the most popular and prestigious schools are having to take steps to ensure that they, rather than their rivals, attract more of the bright children in that area. Putting your bid in at an early age makes sense, always supposing you can tell which the most able children are at the age of four. If the competition for promising four year olds intensifies, some of the boys' all-age schools may decide that they, too, should offer a seamless education.

Among the girls' schools competition is already intense, as more day schools lower the age of entry from seven to four. Heads say this is in response to popular demand but, like American colleges signing up high-school football stars, the schools are fighting to get their hands on the brightest and best of the age group. The boys' schools that have lowered their age of entry are similarly motivated. In some cases they have followed the girls' example and opened nursery schools to recruit at four (or even three); in others, they have settled for a five-year-old entry into a pre-prep school. Some boys' day schools which used to recruit at thirteen have lowered the age of entry to eleven to make it easier for bright children to enter directly from state primary schools. The preparatory schools do not like it but have covered their losses by opening their own pre-prep and nursery departments. Bedales, in Hampshire for example, has a pre-prep department that runs from three to eight; and some all-age schools admit children at two, a practice that gives rise to accusations that mothers – it always seems to be the mother who is blamed – are treating their children like animals.

If you are considering whether an all-age school would be right for your children, you should keep the question of the school's motivation in mind. There is nothing wrong with a school changing its age of entry for economic or competitive reasons, but the head's attempts to persuade you of the educational advantages should be treated with some scepticism. For example, a boys' school that has found it difficult to recruit enough pupils has recently become a fully co-educational school from three to eighteen. Its head is quoted as saying, 'Our integrated learning programme from age three to eighteen underpins stability of education within an exciting quality framework'. That may be a true reflection of what the school has to offer, but in such cases I think you should be careful.

The arguments for and against all-age schools are finely balanced; there are plenty of opinions, but few facts. The academic evidence is equivocal. It would be interesting to know how the products of a seamless education fared in the less-secure world of university and work. But there is some evidence you can ask for when you meet the head. How many pupils leave at sixteen; and, if there is an examination to enter the senior school at eleven or thirteen, how many internal candidates fail and have to go elsewhere?

The choice of any school for your children depends on your judgement of what is best for them. In the case of all-age schools you are being asked to make that judgement when your children are very young. Can you really know when they are four that this will be the right school for them when they are eighteen? It is not an irrevocable commitment, but all-age schools do not make it easy for parents to change their mind when the children are eleven or sixteen; and when it comes to this time, your children may be very reluctant to leave a school where their contemporaries are staying on. If you choose a seamless education when your child is four, you may gain peace of mind but you may also limit your subsequent freedom of choice.

Yours sincerely
John Rae

31 What are the possibilities and risks of switching at the sixth form stage?

Dear Mrs Berenson

The only reason for your daughter to switch at the sixth form stage is to give herself a better chance of good A level grades or access to specialist excellence in, for example, music or sport. Whatever other benefits she may have in mind, such as co-education after being in a single sex school or more freedom after a regime of 'petty restrictions', are not in themselves sufficient reason to change. She may argue that a different social environment will help her to obtain better A levels, but this is unlikely to be true unless the sixth form she is going to has significantly higher academic standards than the one she is leaving.

Her restlessness is understandable; she has been at her present school since the age of four. Even if she had not been, a change of school and teachers for A level appears to have many attractions.

I suggest that you talk through the various options with her as well as the advantages and disadvantages. However, you will have to move quickly because you will need to approach another school or college before your daughter starts her GCSE year in September. Most sixth forms worth considering will hold interviews and, possibly, entrance tests in the first or second term of the GCSE year.

In no particular order, the options are as follows. There are good independent and state schools that admit pupils into the sixth form. But be careful. There are also bad ones which need to fill the gaps created by pupils leaving at GCSE level. This is particularly true of some of the less academic independent boarding schools. Their sixth forms may sound tempting, with scholarships and assisted places available, but unless they offer high academic standards or distinctive excellence in some other field that really does interest your daughter, the temptation should be resisted.

Check the league table to see whether any of the alternative sixth forms within your reach have a better A level record than your daughter's present school. If they do, ask for the school prospectus and the sixth form prospectus which should give you an analysis of A level results subject by subject. You should by now have some idea which A levels your daughter may wish to study and you need to check that the new sixth form offers those subjects to be studied in combination and does well in them.

The advantage of moving to a more high-powered academic sixth form is that the better teaching and the stimulus of talented contemporaries are likely to bring out the best in your daughter. But the sixth form of a leading independent school, such as St Paul's School for Girls or Westminster, is not a place for a girl who lacks confidence, or who is easily disheartened by the culture of success in a competitive environment.

From your point of view, the advantage of a good state school sixth form is that you will not have to pay fees. Some independent schools charge a higher fee for pupils who enter at the sixth form stage so this, too, needs to be part of your calculations.

The disadvantage of moving to another school's sixth form is that your daughter will be entering a close community where friendships have already been made. A new environment may be stimulating, but it will also be alien. Your daughter should not underestimate the difficulty of breaking into an established pattern of relationships, particularly in a single-sex school. It may also be hard for her to adjust to new teachers and new styles of teaching. All these problems can be overcome, but if it takes a term or even two, your daughter will be well into her A level course before she is confident enough to make the best of it. A two-year A level course does not give you the luxury of time to settle down.

The second option is to go to one of the sixth form colleges in the state system. These are not available in all areas – there are none in Inner London for example – but where they do exist they represent a serious challenge to the sixth forms of independent schools. There are no fees. The most successful, such as York Sixth Form College and Hills Road Sixth Form College, in Cambridge, have better A level records than many middle-of-the-road independent schools, though they are not in the same class academically as the independent sector's high flyers. To put that in perspective, at the leading academic independent schools A level candidates average three grade As, at the best sixth form colleges they average BBC and at the middle of the road independent schools they average BCC.

Sixth form colleges are larger than school sixth forms and this enables them to offer a wider range of A level subjects, including those that are not normally available in school sixth forms, such as psychology and media studies. Whether these are advantages I am not sure. A first-year sixth form of between 300 and 500 pupils might be overwhelming – though everyone is new and faces the same problem of adjusting – and the wide choice of A levels could be a trap. Psychology and media studies might seem relevant and refreshingly new compared with what is on offer at her present school, but in the competition for a place at a good university they may be regarded as soft options.

Sixth form colleges are not school sixth forms transferred to another building. They have a style of their own which sometimes hovers uneasily between school and university. The colleges take their pastoral responsibilities seriously, but they pay a price for treating sixteen- and seventeen-year-olds as students. If your daughter is keen to go, I would first check with the principal what the rules are about attending classes and smoking and how they are enforced.

Talk of rules and enforcement will jar on adolescents who are anxious to escape school. But most A level candidates stay at school all the same because they are realists. The days when sixteen- and seventeen-year-olds wanted to stay at school to enjoy the privileges and exercise the power that went with seniority are probably gone for ever. Sixteen- and seventeen-year-olds stay at school now because they know which side their bread is buttered. Their attitude to school rules is one of grudging or amused tolerance. They know their best chance of achieving good A level results and entry into a good university is via their school's sixth form; like ex-patriots working in a backward country, they are prepared to put up with the disagreeable local customs in order to further their career. They recognize that postponing the gratification of a desire – in this case for greater freedom – is likely to be a good investment.

The third option is a further education college. These local colleges offer A levels, but their academic record is poor compared with the other options. Their strength is in vocational subjects and in good links with local employers. They are, however, the least-promising route to a good university.

The fourth option is the private tutorial or crammer. Most were started by educational entrepreneurs who spotted a gap in the market: intensive A level coaching for independent school pupils who had failed the first time, or who had been 'asked to leave', and foreign teenagers who wanted a crash course as a springboard to a British university.

The best tutorials have moved on a long way since they first appeared to become genuine alternatives to school sixth forms and sixth form colleges. From your point of view there are two disadvantages: they are expensive and they cannot provide the level of pastoral care and extra-curricular activities provided by a school. Tuition in three A level subjects will cost more than an independent day school fee. It will cost less than boarding, but you will have the added expenses of your daughter living at home.

The more students there are doing a full two-year A level course, the more the tutorial takes responsibility for the behaviour and whereabouts of its clientele. An easy check on the level of pastoral care, therefore, is to ask what proportion of students are on a two-year course; if they are a minority, look elsewhere. I would also advise against sending your daughter to a tutorial away from home. There are good tutorials with residential provision, notably in Oxford and Cambridge – how tempting they sound – but a tutorial is not a boarding school and I think sixteen is too young to be left largely to your own devices in a sophisticated university city.

The advantages of a tutorial are that your daughter's time-table will be tailored as far as possible to her needs, the teaching groups are small and the whole operation is *focused* on helping her obtain the best possible A level grades. It is this focus that suits some sixteen- and seventeen-year-olds better than the broader educational experience of a school sixth form.

I declare an interest. A number of our own children studied for A level at a private tutorial and it provided just the sort of focused teaching and learning that they needed. I missed their sixth form years at school, but I don't think *they* did. Greater freedom and more responsibility for their own work suited them. Perhaps they were lucky in the tutorial we chose.

The best starting point if you and your daughter are interested in a private tutorial is the Conference for Independent Further Education. The better tutorials are members. That in itself does not guarantee excellence, but it does save you following up every advertisement you see in the newspapers. Some parents assume that when their son or daughter is sixteen and the course is only for two years, they do not need to take so much trouble assessing the different tutorials. That is a mistake. Choosing a tutorial requires as much care as choosing a school.

Your daughter might like to consider a final option of

moving away from the British exam system and taking the International Baccalaureate which is acceptable as a university entrance qualification at British universities. She could combine that with a radical change in educational ethos by applying to Atlantic College in South Wales. There are eight of these United World Colleges around the world. They are genuinely international sixth forms drawing together sixteen- and seventeen-year-olds from many different countries. The ethos is that of Kurt Hahn, the founder of Gordonstoun: it is an exhausting and stimulating journey towards self-discovery, no place for the faint-hearted, but an excellent antidote to the rather self-indulgent lifestyle that characterizes the sixth-form experience in other schools and colleges. But a visit to Atlantic College is essential. The places for home-based applicants are much in demand, so if your daughter is interested you should make contact straightaway.

The secret of a successful transfer at the sixth form stage is not a feeling that it is time for a change, but a *conviction* that your daughter will achieve more in a new environment. Her present headmistress may well discourage a move. It would be wrong to assume, as some parents do, that she is just being obstructive because she does not want to lose a pupil. It is much more likely that she has your daughter's best interests at heart.

On the other hand, if the head *is* being obstructive, as is sometimes the case, you will have to insist that the school supports your daughter's application in a professional manner. The independent sector tries to regulate transfers between schools to prevent poaching, but the Independent Schools Joint Council acknowledges that in the increasingly competitive environment a professional manner may give way to the manners of the market-place.

The decision to move to another sixth form is yours and your daughter's, but you should tread carefully. As one of the best state schools which recruits at eleven says in its prospectus: 'We expect all girls who gain a place at the school to stay with us for seven years'. Your daughter's present school has educated her to the GCSE stage, laying the foundations for her A level years, and will be sad to see another school or college reap the benefit. That is not reason enough to drop the idea of a transfer, but it is a good enough reason to be sensitive to the school's point of view. Being sensitive is all the more important because if your daughter's application to another sixth form is unsuccessful, she may decide that she wishes to stay where she is.

Yours sincerely
John Rae

32 Which are the best state and independent secondary schools and what do they have in common?

Dear Margaret and Stephen

It is impossible to produce a definitive list of the best schools. There would be too many different interpretations of what that superlative means. What I can do is to identify *some* of the schools I think might fall into that category and why, and then see what it is they have in common.

Collating hard evidence is the best place to start. All the criticisms of academic league tables cannot take away from those schools that consistently perform well the right to be considered *among* the best in the country. Over a five-year period, 1992–1996, the most consistently successful schools at A level were Winchester, St Paul's (boys), King Edward's Birmingham, Westminster, Eton, St Paul's (girls) and the North London Collegiate School. I have stopped at seven because that is where the consistency begins to break down. Other schools do well academically, but are not so consistent; others do well by the pupils they admit, adding value in a way that the academic leaders may not, but the hard evidence for their success is lacking.

The seven most consistently successful schools at A level are all independent. The seven most successful state schools at A level are not yet able to threaten the supremacy of these independent schools, but nevertheless they are among the best schools in the country because they are producing good A level results in less favourable circumstances. They are as selective academically as the top independent schools, but they do not have the financial resources to provide their pupils with such small classes, or such extensive and up-to-date facilities. Over the same five-year period, 1992–1996, the seven most consistently successful state schools at A level were the Royal Grammar School, High Wycombe, Chelmsford County High School for Girls, King Edward VI Grammar School, Chelmsford, Newstead Wood School for Girls, Bromley, the Judd School, Tonbridge, Colchester County High School for Girls, and Henrietta Barnett School, North London.

All of these fourteen schools, whose claim to be among the best is based on success at A level, are single sex; Westminster admits some girls to the sixth form, but remains in essence a single-sex school. With the exception of King Edward's, Birmingham, all these schools are in the south of England and within commuting distance of London. There are academically successful state and independent schools in the north, particularly in Greater Manchester, but based on their consistent A level performance the southern schools have the edge.

Five of the seven state schools are grant maintained schools, having opted out of local authority control; a sixth is considering doing so. Only two of the fourteen – Winchester and Eton – are fully boarding schools.

Before you jump to the conclusion that single sexness is the most obvious factor that the best schools have in common, I will add to this list the two most successful schools in the Scottish Higher exam; they are Hutchesons' Grammar School, Glasgow, and Glasgow High School, both of which are fully co-educational independent schools.

In fact, what these sixteen schools do have in common is that they are *successful*, and in education, as in other things, nothing succeeds like success. But it would be wrong to suppose that all these schools have to do is to select the most able children for good A level results to follow. A school cannot sustain a high academic standard, however selective its intake, unless it is running a very efficient operation. If the operation falters as a result of changing circumstances or poor leadership, the school soon loses its position among the leading academic schools. Thirty years ago, the only academic league tables available showed the percentage of sixth formers winning scholarships to Oxford and Cambridge. Some of the schools that figured prominently in those tables have adapted to the different demands of A level, but others have simply faded from prominence. Dulwich College in South London, for example, was for many years number two in the scholarship table, but now it cannot make the top fifty at A level.

The rise and fall of individual schools is one reason why there is still strong resistance among heads to the ranking of schools by academic performance. But using other criteria to identify schools that are 'among the best' is even less popular. What I have done is to select those schools that are leaders in their field, or that have successfully developed a distinctive ethos or excellence which has strong appeal to parents. The majority of these schools are independent; partly because I know the independent schools better, but it is also because it is more difficult for individual state schools to stand out from the rest. Being distinctive requires a remarkably strong-minded head, or a degree of freedom that only those state schools that have opted out of local control are likely to enjoy.

The London Oratory School opted out and has been led for twenty years by a singularly determined head. A single-sex boys' Roman Catholic school, with some girls in the sixth form, it is among the best state comprehensive schools in the country. The headmaster, John McIntosh, has created the school in its present form, demonstrating that an inner-city comprehensive can stimulate the brightest – there are more former London Oratory pupils at Oxford than from most independent schools – *and* develop high morale and good discipline.

The London Oratory is not a community school; it is fed by 146 primary schools from all over London. St Louise's Comprehensive College in the Falls Road, Belfast, is a community school; because it involves and is involved in the local community with such conspicuous success, I think it is among the best schools in the United Kingdom. It must surely be the only school where 99 per cent of parents come to parents meetings. A state Roman Catholic school in a very deprived area, it has 2300 girls between the ages of eleven and eighteen and is the largest single-sex school in Western Europe.

It, too, in its present form is the creation of a strong-minded and highly influential head, Sister Genevieve of the Order of St Vincent de Paul, who was Principal from 1963–1988.

St Louise's is another example of an inner-city comprehensive transformed by inspired leadership. At first sight, the outstanding independent Roman Catholic school, Ampleforth College, the Benedictine foundation in Yorkshire, is a very different sort of school. Remote from the inner city, selective academically and serving a middle-class clientele, Ampleforth nevertheless has in common with both St Louise's and the London Oratory the ability to realize an asset. Many schools have a religious affiliation, both Roman Catholic and Protestant, but only a few make such good use of the shared religious faith and the shared values between home and school as does Ampleforth.

The leading co-educational school is King's School, Canterbury. It is among the best because it has so skilfully adapted a single-sex tradition with roots in the early middle ages to the demands of a high-powered, co-educational school that produces better academic results than any of its co-educational rivals whether state or independent.

The most successful sporting school is Millfield School in Somerset. Other schools excel at one sport; Millfield excels at most. Sporting excellence reflects the school's distinctive and expensive approach to education. Whatever the child is good or bad at, the school will provide the help that is needed. So there is professional coaching for dyslexics as well as sporting stars.

A different, but equally distinctive, vision of what education

should be about also puts Gordonstoun among the best. So-
called progressive schools outside the mainstream have usually
lacked staying power, as the vision of the founder faded
or mainstream schools adopted the progressive ideas.
Gordonstoun is the exception. Kurt Hahn's vision of an education, in which practical service to the community and a real
spirit of adventure are not just extra-curricular activities but
central to the life of the school, is alive and well though it is
having to adapt to a world in which academic qualifications
matter. Gordonstoun girls and boys still learn seamanship during morning school – rowing a deep lug cutter out of the
harbour and into the swell – while their contemporaries at
other schools are sitting in class. Gordonstoun is aware of the
market, but refuses to pander to it. If any progressive school
can retain its distinctive vision and still meet the rising academic aspirations of pupils and their parents, Gordonstoun is
the one to do so.

In addition, I could have short-listed other schools from
among those state schools that are classified as 'outstandingly
successful secondary schools' by the chief inspector in his
annual report, or from among those independent boarding
schools, such as Radley or St Mary's, Calne, which excel academically without the highly selective intake of the independent day schools. But the twenty-two I have chosen are
sufficiently varied to give us some idea what it is that the best
schools might have in common.

Nineteen of the twenty-two are fully independent, or have
opted out of local authority control. The significant distinction
between secondary schools is not between those which charge
fees and those that do not, but between those which have the
freedom to run their own affairs and those that are still subject
to the local education authority. The latter may include some
very good schools, such as the Judd School and Henrietta
Barnett, but the fact remains that what the great majority of
outstanding secondary schools have in common is that they
are masters of their own fate or, to put it another way, they

are free from interference by people whose motives owe more to politics than education.

Seventeen of the twenty-two are single sex, but I would not attach too much importance to that. In Scotland where co-education is well established, the best schools are likely to be co-educational; in England where co-education, particularly in the independent sector, is comparatively new, it is unremarkable that many of the best schools are single sex. On the other hand, I think it is interesting that only one of the twenty-two schools – Gordonstoun – has fewer than six hundred pupils and that the average number of pupils is nine hundred. At the secondary level, smaller is not necessarily better.

The characteristics that some of these schools share are not as important, however, as the one feature which they *all* have in common. Every successful school has a clear vision of what it is trying to achieve. It does not matter whether that vision is made explicit, or is taken for granted. Some of these schools will tell you what their vision is, others would never use the word, but it is their common denominator nevertheless. It gives them a sense of direction. Do you remember a film called '*I know where I'm going*'? When I spend time in one of these schools and listen to its voice, that is what I hear.

For some of these successful schools, the vision is in the tradition; they know where they are going because they have always known. Winchester has been a centre of learning and scholarship for six hundred years and that it is still one of the most successful academic schools in the country is testimony to the power of its own tradition. In other cases, the vision is a modern creation, the work of an idealistic founder – Kurt Hahn of Gordonstoun, Jack Meyer of Millfield – or of an inspirational head such as John McIntosh or Sister Genevieve. Others again find their vision and sense of direction not in long established tradition, or inspirational leadership, but in the steady accumulation of success which creates its own dynamic of high expectations.

The vision of a school – of what it is about and where it is going – is not the same as the development plan, though the inspectors sometimes confuse the two; as in, 'The School has not formulated a clear enough vision of its future and insufficient attention is given to systematic development planning'. What places Winchester and the London Oratory, the North London Collegiate School and St Louise's Comprehensive College among the best schools in the country is not 'systematic development planning', but a distinctive ethos, an educational ideal.

Systematic planning is important but it is the vision, not the planning, which provides the motivation for all those other elements that make schools effective – the unity of purpose, the pride in doing things well, the high expectations, the efficient organization, the good discipline and the orderly atmosphere.

There has never been any secret about what constitutes a good school, but without imagination the elements are lifeless. In a school without vision, unity of purpose is just a phrase on the headmaster's lips; you can hear him addressing the staff in mid-morning break on how important it is for everyone to pull together and you can imagine the expressions on the faces of his audience. School teachers are notoriously difficult to inspire with a common sense of purpose – at times they seem to delight in pulling in different directions – but where there is a vision and a clear sense of direction even the most individualistic or idiosyncratic teachers work towards the same end. The contrast between the staff room in a school which knows where it is going and one that does not is immediately obvious. The former is animated, the latter is slumped into its tattered armchair in a posture of permanent defeat. It is the lack of this vision, rather than the lack of resources, that holds many schools back.

It takes a remarkable head to turn round a defeated school and there is a sense in which the better the school the less it needs that quality of leadership. The vision and the sense of direction are already there. What most of the good schools need and usually appoint is an accomplished professional who is in sympathy with the vision and who will keep the school focused upon it. But turning round a defeated school, or creating an outstanding school, as Sister Genevieve has, for example, in the Falls Road, Belfast – where unemployment stretches back three generations – requires something more than professionalism. It calls for a touch of greatness, which I think Sister Genevieve possessed.

You ask what the best state and independent schools have in common. What they do not necessarily have in common is inspiring head teachers. They have the head they need to do the job. It would be too much to hope that for all those schools that *do* need inspired leadership, a John McIntosh or a Sister Genevieve could be found, but at least those who appoint head teachers to these schools should be looking for something more than managerial competence. If the head cannot provide the vision and sense of direction, who can?

Yours sincerely
John Rae

33 What future changes may affect our children's education?

Dear Emily

One thing you can be sure of is that wherever the political power lies the determination to make schools more publicly accountable will not slacken. Ideology is not dead, but there is a rare political consensus on the need to develop practical and realistic ways of improving individual schools. The national curriculum, national testing of pupils, the publication of test and exam results, the regular inspection of schools and the rewarding of good teachers while weeding out the bad, will be part of any future government's education policy.

That is good news for Lucy and Katie because public accountability is already proving to be an effective way of bringing out the best in schools, despite opposition to this system from within. The heads of state and independent schools are united in their hostility to league tables, though in the case of some independent heads this is mere hypocrisy or, to put it more kindly, solidarity with their weaker brethren. Some teachers' unions are opposed to procedures for identifying good and bad teachers and some school governors are so opposed to national tests that they refuse to hand over the results.

Teachers are bound to resent the suggestion that they need public accountability to keep them up to the mark, but it is in their own interests that their performance should be seen to be openly assessed. Teaching is not like marketing, for example; it cannot be assessed in sales figures. But neither is it a mystery beyond measurement. Schools could have targets appropriate to their intake, and there is no reason why a teacher's performance should not be rated – just like any other worker who aspires to be treated as a professional. The establishment of a General Teaching Council to regulate high professional standards would help both teachers and pupils and there is a good chance that this will come into being while your children are still at school.

But while I expect Lucy and Katie to benefit from the determination to improve individual schools, my optimism is not without reservation because I am aware that the ideological battles that have bedevilled education for the last thirty years are not yet over. Selection for schools, streaming in schools, competition between schools and between pupils, even competitive sports are still anathema to those who believe that school must not highlight or encourage inequalities. Support for this egalitarian philosophy has waned over the years, not least because it has become synonymous with low expectations, but in one respect it remains a strong force.

Academic selection for entry to secondary schools is still fiercely opposed, particularly by the Labour Party. New Labour can come to terms with streaming by ability, league tables and competitive sport but not with academic selection, as the furore over Harriet Harman's decision to send her son to a selective state school confirmed. But the political advocates of academic selection, particularly in the Conservative Party, are no less passionate in their determination to see this practice retained and, if possible, extended.

This conflict, ideological as well as political, could affect your children's education in a number of ways. If a Labour government outlawed selection that would not automatically deny your children good academic education on the state, but it would limit your choice. Of the top fifty state schools in the 1996 A level league tables, forty are academically selective. Whether New Labour will force these schools to become comprehensive or merely ban any *further* academic selection in state schools is not clear.

Half of the top one hundred state schools at A level are grant maintained and their heads argue that their success owes as much to the greater freedom they enjoy, as to the academic selection that most of them practise. But uncertainty about selection makes it difficult to predict whether these schools – now to be called 'foundation schools' – will continue to offer a good academic education.

One of the beneficiaries of Labour's hostility to selection schools will be the weaker independent school. Just when the state schools are mounting a successful challenge to the independent schools on the question that matters most to parents – good academic standards – Labour looks set to give the most vulnerable independent schools a reprieve by reducing the state sector competition. But the reprieve is only likely to be temporary. There will not be enough parents who are willing to pay boarding fees to a school whose only selling point is that it is not the local comprehensive.

Before Katie leaves school in about seventeen years' time, I expect between forty and fifty of the most vulnerable independent schools to either close or merge. That may sound a lot, but it is only two or three a year and so that number may turn out to be a conservative estimate, particularly if the schools have to bear unexpected costs, such as increased contributions to the pensions of teachers who retire early. This reduction will limit your choice over time and will make the better independent schools even harder to get into.

The ending of the assisted places scheme, which is on Labour's agenda, *will* also limit your choice. For parents who cannot afford the full fees, this route into independent education will be closed. The effect on the independent schools themselves will be profound. The schools will tend to play down the loss of pupils and will instead insist that they will have little difficulty recruiting other pupils of similar calibre. But they will have to find thirty thousand pupils – enough to fill thirty large secondary schools – whose parents can pay the full fees. The stronger academic schools may well manage, but only by taking fee paying pupils from the weaker schools who will thus suffer a double loss.

Labour's policies may also limit your choice by making independent schools more expensive. That will not necessarily be true because of the ending of the assisted places scheme – unless the schools continue to subsidize some pupils out of fee income – but it is true of the loss of charitable status which would increase fees by 5 per cent to 10 per cent. So if you are budgeting for the possibility of having to pay fees at some stage of your children's education, it would be as well to build these considerations into your figures. There are now numerous companies and consultants eager to tell you how to plan ahead for the payment of school fees, but I should start by seeking the advice of the Independent Schools Information Service.

You may think I have interpreted the impact of Labour's policies from too narrow a viewpoint. The ending of the assisted places scheme will also make money available to reduce the size of classes in primary schools, and both this policy and the ending of selection should ensure that comprehensive schools are more truly comprehensive with a stronger intake of more able children. But the actual improvement in primary and secondary schools may be very gradual while the impact on your *choice* could be immediate.

While I am confident that the drive to make schools and teachers more publicly accountable will continue, I am less certain of how the effects of each party's political agendas for the education system will work out. Both major political parties believe their policies are designed, like public accountability, to improve individual schools. The Conservatives favour extending academic selection, doubling the number of pupils on the assisted places scheme and encouraging more schools to opt out of local control to become grant maintained. Labour favours restricting academic selection, ending the assisted places scheme and is ambivalent towards grant maintained schools.

But how many policies in education have the result their authors intended? Few people would have predicted in 1965, when Labour came to power with a large majority and a commitment to bring independent schools under state control, that thirty years later these schools would be still enjoying their independence and that the best of them would be overflowing with pupils and confidence. All *you* can do is to be aware of what changes are on the cards and ensure that your plans are flexible. This is no time to pin your hopes on a single solution to the problem of where to send your children to school.

There are other changes, already under way, whose development does not depend on politicians and which will affect your role as a parent, as well as Lucy and Katie's education. The two which seem to me the most significant are the impact of information technology on the way children learn and the increasing emphasis on parents' responsibilities.

Your children's schooldays will be enlivened by the debate on how far information technology will enable pupils to be less dependent on teachers and less tied to the classroom. Don't be alarmed by those who say that the new technology is on a collision course with conventional education and that schools will soon disappear. That is headline-grabbing futurology. Information technology is just giving a new twist to an old debate about how and when to wean pupils from becoming over dependent on teachers.

When the whole of the *Encyclopaedia Britannica* is on a few CDs, the possibilities for independent work at a young age are obvious, and not just for the brighter pupils. Information technology can be a powerful motivator for children whose first reaction to a teacher in the classroom is to switch off. I do not expect Lucy and Katie's generation to 'work from home', but I do expect them to spend more time doing their own research and, as they move up the school, spend more time directing their own work and less time being told what to do. And as the old debate is given this new impetus, you will inevitably be drawn in, not least because you will be required to understand the technology that Lucy and Katie are using with such facility.

You will be involved in an equally lively debate about the division of labour between home and school on such issues as morals and manners. The trend over the last two decades has been to expect schools to provide a cure for more and more of society's ills. That trend will soon be reversed as society becomes disenchanted with the idea that schools are effective instruments for inculcating attitudes and values. Just how responsibility will be passed back to the home is not at all clear, though the introduction of increasingly detailed contracts between school and parents is one possibility.

Some years ago, a primary school headmistress told me that the mother of a new girl expected the school to teach her daughter how to tie her shoelaces. 'That's what I send her to school to learn.' Parents of tomorrow's pupils should no longer assume that the schools will take the lead responsibility for teaching children to be well mannered, to be good citizens, to know the difference between right and wrong, to respect others, to learn self-discipline, to understand religion, and eventually to be good parents themselves. Schools will never abandon their responsibility for teaching values and educating the whole person, but in the coming years both schools and society will expect more of parents in all these areas. I do not imagine that will cause you any dismay because you never intended to be an innocent bystander in relation to your children's education, but it will come as an unwelcome surprise to those parents, in all walks of life, who send their children to school to learn the moral equivalent of tying their shoelaces.

Perhaps the most important thing to keep in mind when you are thinking about all these possible changes is that while a successful strategy for Lucy and Katie's education depends on your being well informed, anxiety can throw your strategy off course as easily as ignorance. It is natural for parents to worry about their children's education but some parents become too concerned. They think they should change their plans every time they come across a new piece of information about a school or read about a new piece of research, but the majority of this information turns out to be hearsay or gossip and most educational research can safely be ignored.

The future will not look after itself; you do need to plan Lucy and Katie's education, and to base your plans on as much hard evidence as you can obtain. But at a time when education is so fully reported and discussed in the media, you will also need to keep your nerve and trust your own judgement.

Yours sincerely
John Rae

AFTERWORD

Our schooldays have a lasting effect on us for good or ill. While there are successful people who say they owe nothing to their education, and determined people who return to education as adults to obtain good degrees in middle age, having left school at sixteen without a single qualification, these people are the exception. It is possible to recover from a poor education, though it is not easy; and for everyone who overcomes the handicap of bad schooling there must be many more who are permanently discouraged and who never discover what they might have been had they experienced the benefits of a good and rounded education.

So parents are right to move heaven and earth to ensure that their children go to good schools to receive the best possible education. The problem is knowing how to keep a sense of proportion when so much is at stake. The pressure on parents is increased by what must appear to be the unfairness of the British system. Why should access to good schools depend on where you live, what church you attend, or what you can afford? It is the knowledge that some really good state and independent schools do exist and that if you can get your child into one of them it may make all the difference to his or her life, that keeps many British parents awake at night.

It is natural for parents to worry about their children's education. But parents know that they must prevent their deep-seated concern about their children's education becoming so obsessional that it distorts their lives and their children's lives in the process.

In my experience, when parents lose their sense of proportion about their children's schooling, it is almost always because they mistake or substitute their own ambitions for their children's best interests. For example, I recall meeting with parents whose son had failed the Westminster entrance exam and realizing that they were just as worried about loss of face in their social circle as they were about their son's future.

Being able to hold your head high among your friends and neighbours is a thoroughly bad reason for wanting your child to win a place at a particular school. It encourages unrealistic goals. The best school in the neighbourhood, or the most sought-after independent school, may be beyond a particular child's reach, yet it is typical of parents who are thinking only of their own social criteria or academic pretensions that they insist that their child sits the entrance exam and then, when their child fails, complain loudly about injustice. You can imagine what that does to their child's level of confidence and self-esteem.

Even when parents are certain they are acting selflessly in planning their children's education – concentrating all their efforts on finding the school most suited to their child's requirements – they may still worry that some of the methods they use are disproportionate. I believe they worry unnecessarily. When the schools available are so uneven in quality, extra coaching, practice exams, attempts to lay hands on last year's papers, moving house and rediscovering a long-forgotten religious commitment are all perfectly legitimate tactics to employ.

It is less easy, however, to advise parents on how much academic pressure it is wise to place on a child of four, or seven, or eleven. We probably underestimate the capacity of fairly young children for hard work and, indeed, their willingness to pit their wits against their peers. Parents probably underestimate, too, their children's ability to cope at interviews. Interviewing many seven- and thirteen-year-olds, I found that the most impressive were always those whose natural liveliness had not been curbed by too much parental coaching.

Of course, there are some children who need encouragement rather than challenge, and one-to-one tuition as opposed to practice exams; as there are others whose enthusiasm for work is almost fanatical and who need to learn how to relax and to find pleasure in childish things. But the majority of children, certainly those approaching secondary school age, are more resilient and tougher mentally than some educationalists give them credit for. I doubt whether those who have had to make sacrifices to win a place at a good school feel the strain as much as their parents do. Nor do I think they regret the loss of carefree days. Why should we assume that the less we demand of children the happier they will be? As long as parents keep their anxieties to themselves, I see no reason whatsoever why the sacrifice needed to do well in education should make children or young people unhappy. On the contrary, the sense of achievement when hard work or training produces good results is a great boost to a young person's morale.

Happiness, anyway, is a concept we should consider with caution in relation to schooldays. 'Children learn best when they are happy,' says a preparatory school prospectus. It is difficult to quarrel with that, but the learning process will not always be enjoyable. Sometimes it will be frustrating, difficult or plain boring. Nor are our schooldays 'the happiest days of our lives'. It is rewarding to see boys and girls having fun at school – which most of them do some of the time, but few, if any, do all the time. I am a little sceptical when the historian H. A. L. Fisher tells us, 'I enjoyed every moment of my life at Winchester'. Parents should not fall into the trap of believing that their strategy has gone awry, or that they are putting too much pressure on their children to do well, if their child's schooldays are not always a smooth and happy path into adulthood.

What of the parents' happiness and peace of mind? There must be times when parents ask themselves whether getting their children into a good school is worth the emotional strain it sometimes causes. If the chosen school is a disappointment, or if the element of chance gives their child a raw deal, they may go on asking themselves the same question throughout the course of their child's school years. The answer will always be the same. The effort required to ensure your children have a good education is worthwhile whatever the outcome. My advice to all parents when faced with these important decisions would be the same as theirs to a child on the morning of an exam: 'Just do your best, that's what really matters'.

APPENDIX
Useful Addresses

1 Boarding Schools Association
(BSA)
Ysgol Nant,
Valley Road,
Llanfairfechan,
Gwynedd, LL33 0ES

01248 680542

2 British Dyslexia Association
98 London Road,
Reading, RG1 5AU

01734 668271

3 Catholic Education Council
for England and Wales
41 Cromwell Road,
London SW7 2DJ

0171 584 7491

4 Conference of Independent
Further Education (CIFE)
Buckhall Farm,
Bull Lane,
Bethersden,
Near Ashford,
Kent, TN26 3HB

01233 820797

5 Department for Education
and Employment (DFEE)
Sanctuary Buildings,
Great Smith Street,

Westminster,
London SW1P 3BT

0171 925 5000 (for School
Curriculum Branch
0171 925 5726)

6 Dyslexia Institute
133 Gresham Road,
Staines,
Middlesex, TW18 2AJ

01784 463851

7 Girls Public Day School Trust
26 Queen Anne's Gate,
London SW1

0171 222 9595

8 Girls Schools Association
(GSA)
130 Regent Road,
Leicester, LE1 7PG

0116 2471797

9 Grant Maintained Schools
Centre
Red Lion House,
9–10 High Street,
High Wycombe, HP11 2AZ

01494 474470

10   Headmasters' and Headmistresses' Conference
(HMC)
130 Regent Road,
Leicester, LE1 7PG

0116 2854810

11   Incorporated Association of
Preparatory Schools (IAPS)
11 Waterloo Place,
Leamington Spa,
Warwickshire, CV32 5LA

01926 887833

12   Independent Schools Information Service (ISIS)
56 Buckingham Gate,
London SW1E 6AG

0171 630 8793/4

13   ISIS Scotland
11 Castle Street,
Edinburgh, EH2 3AH

0131 220 2106

14   Institute for the Study of
Drug Dependence (ISDD)
Waterbridge House,
32–36 Loman Street,
London SE1 0EE

0171 928 1211

15   National Association for
Gifted Children (NAGC)
Park Campus,
Boughton Green Road,
Northampton, NN2 7AL

01604 792300

16   National Confederation of
Parent–Teachers Associations
48 Hammerton Road,
Gravesend

01474 560618

17   Office for Standards in Edu-
cation (OFSTED)
Alexandra House,
Kingsway,
London WC2

0171 421 6800

For OFSTED publications:
PO Box 6927,
London E3 3NZ

0171 510 0180

18   Parents National Education
Union
Strode House,
44 Osnaburgh Street,
London NW1

0171 387 9228

19   Round Square Conference
Schools
Secretary,
Box Hill School,
Dorking,
Surrey, RH5 6EA

20   Society of Headmasters and
Headmistresses of Indepen-
dent Schools (SHMIS)
Celedston,
Rhosemor Road,
Halkyn,
Holywell, CH8 8DL

01352 781102

21 State Boarding Information
    Service (STABIS)
    Contact the Boarding Schools
    Association

INDEX

A levels 96
  combinations 96–7
  location of head on publishing of
    results 101
  see also league tables
Aberdeen Grammar School 60
academic league tables *see* league
  tables
academic success 3–4
  change in view of 4–5
  emphasis on 6–7, 24, 25–6, 180,
    181
accountability 231–2, 234
addresses, useful 243–5
alcohol misuse 126, 147–53
all-age schools 14–15, 57, 59,
  211–15
American schools 47
Ampleforth College 45, 171–2, 178,
  226
Anglican independent schools 170, 172
Ardingly 133
area
  good education dependent on 16, 17
Arnold, Thomas 107
assisted places scheme 11, 17–20, 21,
  233–4
Atlantic College (South Wales) 221

'bad year', phenomenon of 64
Bedales 214
Benedictine schools 169
Bishop's Stortford College 170
boarding schools xii, 121–30, 198–9
  academic success 53

advantages of good 127–8
age of entry 128
bullying 155, 157
changes in 125
characteristics of bad 127, 128
co-education 129
counselling 126
criticism of 124–5
drinking 126, 148–9, 150, 151, 152
drugs 145
flexibility 128–9
greater independence claim 124
importance of choice of housemaster
  64
importance of efficiency and
  professionalism 130
lawlessness on campus 125–6
in lower half of league tables 7, 198
motives for sending to 122
provision of fuller education 123–4
in Scotland 58–9, 60
shrinking in market 11, 53, 128
sixth forms 217
and state schools 121, 122, 129–30
visit to 76, 85–6
Boarding Schools Association 130
Boateng, Paul 36
bright children *see* gifted children
British Crime Survey 140
Buckinghamshire 16
buildings 83
bullying xiii, 154–9
  forms of 156
  importance of discipline in
    countering 156–7, 158–9